M000170276

# About the Author

Frankie McNamara is the brains behind the popular Meditations for The Anxious Mind Instagram account, which gained a cult following by making hilarious videos about iconic locations in Ireland. He has amassed over 180,000 followers on Instagram and TikTok combined. This is his first book.

Meditations for the
Anxious Mind

*PRESENTS*

# THE TOXIC TRAVEL GUIDE

## Ireland as You've Never Seen it Before

HarperCollins*Ireland*

Harper Ireland
Macken House,
39/40 Mayor Street Upper,
Dublin 1
D01 C9W8

a division of
HarperCollins*Publishers*
1 London Bridge Street
London SE1 9GF
UK

www.harpercollins.co.uk

First published by HarperCollinsIreland in 2022

1 3 5 7 9 10 8 6 4 2

All photographs courtesy of Alamy

catalogue record of this book is available from the British Library

HB ISBN 978-0-00-852707-5

ₐTypeset by Palimpsest Book Production Ltd, Falkirk, Stirlingshire

Printed and bound in the UK using 100% renewable electricity
at CPI Group (UK) Ltd

MIX
Paper | Supporting
responsible forestry
FSC www.fsc.org    FSC™ C007454

*I'd like to dedicate this book to myself.*
*Without me, none of this would be possible, obviously.*
*Namaste.*

# CONTENTS

# INTRODUCTION

Hello, I'm Frankie. Thank you for tuning in to meditations for the anxious mind. Although it cannot be confirmed or denied, I've had the unfortunate pleasure of living thousands of lives. So I decided to write a travel guide to document my findings. Despite the fact that my past-life regression skills are perhaps my most impressive quality, much of my research has been corroborated by the insights of my followers. And when I say followers, I'm not talking about social media. I'm talking about followers in the truest sense of the word. I'm a cult leader.

And I'm thinking of getting into forex trading.

This travel guide seeks to explore the unexplored side of Ireland. An unnecessary task perhaps, but somebody had to do it. Somebody had to talk about Laois. Somebody had to unLaois the beast. Within this book you'll find a definitive guide to each county in Ireland along with a few of the must-see attractions, however don't actually go to any of these places. They look far better in this book than they do in real life. Honestly, Ireland is a bit of a kip. I feel at home here.

This travel guide will not only teach you about Ireland, it may reveal some truths about yourself. You might not be ready to hear them. But don't worry. You can't hear words that are written in book format, you can only see them. Unless you bought the audiobook, in which case, shit one.

Anyway, I hope this book makes money. Clearly that's the only reason I'm writing a book. If it flops, maybe you could give us a fiver next time you see me, out of pity. Pity fivers still look the same in my wallet. When you are finished with this book please sell it to your friend for a mark-up and send me the cost price via bank transfer. That way, if you make money, I make money, and that's what meditation is all about! If you don't have any friends, just bury your copy of the book in a hole in your back garden for your future grandchildren/archaeologists to excavate in years to come, so that my legacy may be immortalised.

There are many nooks and crannies to be found in the underbelly of Irish culture. Many of them fascinating, most of them disgusting, all of them found in these pages.

Sorry about that.

Namaste.

# COUNTY ANTRIM

Antrim is a hub of artists. These artists don't paint standing up. They only paint kerbs. Due to the shortage of available colours in Antrim they can only use red, white and blue. Antrim is full of Loyalists. Everyone thinks Loyalists are people who believe they're from the United Kingdom, but Loyalists are actually just people who eat English breakfasts and have loads of money because they manifested a reality where they think they're related to the Queen. Then there's Belfast. Belfast thinks it should be its own country just because they have a train station. Antrim hates beautiful scenery. The people here don't like dealing with concepts that don't fit into words. This is why they call everything Glen. There are nine mountain valleys and they just called them all Glen. Who's Glen?

# Top five things you don't want to miss:

## 1. Asda
Asda is basically just Tesco of the North. The only difference is that you never see Catholics and Protestants playing hide-and-seek with each other in Tesco. I wish.

## 2. The Giant's Causeway
The Giant's Causeway is a great spot to go to if you love rock formations and revel at the sight of disappointed tourists that come to the sudden realisation that there are no giants here. Which is great. Giants are scary. This is also the place for you if getting ripped off turns you on. It's ten pounds for a parking space.

## 3. Ulster Aviation Society
This is the place to be if you like getting your hopes up. Have fun with your friends and tell them you found a way to fly out of Antrim, then bring them here and make them stare at fighter jets in a museum of WWII memorabilia.

## 4. Antrim coast
The Antrim coast is a great place to go if you want to interrupt people trying to take Instagram pictures of the sunset.

## 5. The constant flooding
Make sure to imbibe yourself in the local culture and witness the great floods of Antrim, which happen about every two weeks. It's the only time the natives of Antrim wash themselves.

**TOXICITY RATING: 7.5**

# Belfast

Belfast is a city made up of five quarters because people from Belfast can't count, they think 26+6=1. Belfast is the biggest city in Ireland, when you don't count all the other cities that are bigger than Belfast, like Dublin. Everyone from Belfast thinks being from Belfast is a personality type. Belfast is the Cork city of Northern Ireland. People from North Belfast sleep for eighteen hours a day and only open their window to shout across the road at their neighbour. They wander around the Cathedral Quarter in their pyjamas all year round and can often fall asleep standing up. Everyone in Belfast brags about the *Titanic* like they built it, and like it didn't sink on its first voyage. They even have a museum to celebrate this failure, over a hundred years later.

## Urban myths and legends

The Catholic and Protestant areas of West Belfast are separated by peace walls. They're the least peaceful places on the planet. Since the fire that burnt down the Primark in 2018, all the millies and smicks have been walking around Belfast without any clothes on.

Everyone has been confused by the statue of a big fish in the heart of the city centre. It's finally been revealed that Gerry Adams lives inside here. Every time the fish gets kissed by the lips of a Protestant, the North moves a step further away from a unified Ireland, but when the reality of a 32-county Ireland arrives, Gerry will go back into the lake and go for a really long backstroke, because if there's one thing Gerry Adams loves doing on his days off, it's going for a really good swim.

Everyone gets confused by the Orange Order, but it's not that difficult. They're a group of men from Belfast who wear Scottish garments, marching in the name of a Dutch king under an English flag. In Belfast, the Orange men are everywhere, but we never hear of the Apple men or the Banana men. Where's their parade? It's 2022, all fruits deserve equal rights.

## Local cuisine

The famous delicacy of Belfast is the Belfast bap, which is just a breakfast roll with the baguette substituted for two huge burnt loaves of crusty bread, dusted with flour. This local sandwich was socially engineered by the government to be so big that Belfastians would spend most of their lives trying to fit it in their mouths, which meant they wouldn't be talking in their loud voices and scaring away the pigeons. When a group of three or more Belfastians congregate to eat a Belfast bap, this is known as a Belfeast.

## NIGHTLIFE

The Jailhouse is one of the most loved pubs in Belfast. The toilets in the Jailhouse are a five-minute walk away from the bar, because as much as the staff here want you to have a good time, they also want you to exercise.

In the Cathedral Quarter everyone goes to the Harp Bar to drink, even though it's impossible to get a pint there because they're always overcrowded and under-staffed. It's believed that there are some people in there now that are still waiting on a drink, and they got there before the Good Friday Agreement.

Namaste.

## Glenarm

Glenarm is a small village in county Antrim. Glenarm in English translates to 'valley of the army'. Despite its name, no one has seen a military presence here as of late, because Glenarm is a sanctuary of peace and love. They say magic mushrooms grow out of the bus stops here, and the wheels on the bus are made out of marshmallows and hope. Antrim was invented by some random narcissist called Glen who kept naming everything after himself. Besides Glenarm, there's Glencloy, Glenariffe, Glencorp, Glenballyemon, Glenann, Glendun, Glenshesk and Glentaisie. Glen is set to build a tenth Glen-based village in Antrim in the next five years. It will be a micro-climate full of people who love doing the sunbeds and lack the self-esteem to go on *Love Island*. Reports speculate it will be known as 'Glenerife'.

## Urban myths and legends

A few miles south of Glenarm, there's a strange assortment of limescale rocks overlooking the harbour, it's known as the Madman's Window.

Legend has it that it got its name after a woman drowned in the bay, it's believed her grieving husband used to go out there every subsequent day and stare blankly at the sea to masturbate. The natives of Glenarm are generally a peaceful bunch, and they are totally against weapons. Unless the weapons are stones, they love keeping stones in their pocket for protection. So no traditional weapons are used in Glenarm but when it comes to stones, everyone is Glenarmed to the teeth.

Glenarm Forest is one of the most cherished enclaves of natural life in the area. This little forest used to be the private property of Glenarm Castle, where the Earl of Antrim still resides to this day, but because the Earl of Antrim plays *FIFA 06* on his brand new PlayStation 2 all day, he never leaves his castle to go outside so he decided to make his garden a public space. There's a stunning lake in the forest where the locals like to go fishing. Although all they ever catch is salmon, which upsets the people to no end, because the only fish people from Glenarm will eat is out of a chipper. So they all go down to their local takeaway and deep fry the salmon and pretend they're eating something that actually tastes good.

There's a jewellers in Glenarm by the name of Steenson's. They make the jewellery for the *Game of Thrones* franchise. Legend has it that the owner thinks the business is also in *Game of Thrones*. He believes an invisible camera crew have been deployed to survey their every move. This is why the staff go around wearing crowns and pendants and use terms like 'my lord' or 'my lady' while also wearing really luxurious dressing gowns.

## NIGHTLIFE

In Glenarm, there's a bar called the Bridge End Tavern, more commonly known as 'Stevie's' which is the name of the owner. They believe in the prompt service of cheap, delicious pints combined with a pick-and-mix sweets stand in the corner for the kids who got dragged to the pub by their drunk parents so they don't have to sit at home with them and watch *Peppa Pig*. Instead they get to watch Drunk Pig; a one-man tragic comedy show starring their own father.

Namaste.

# COUNTY ARMAGH

Armagh stands at the foothold of communism in Ireland. Armagh believes in the equal distribution of everyone's Ma. When you come to Armagh, your Ma is no longer your Ma, it's Armagh. Armagh is the Mi Wadi of human ownership. Armagh is famous for its cider production. It's known as the Orchard County. The Armaghians have a secret religion where they drink flagons of cider all day just to experience a hangover cure the next morning: more cider.

# Top five things you don't want to miss:

## 1. Bagel beans
Bagel beans are a local delicacy in Armagh. This is because no one in Armagh knows how to cook for themselves. They love it so much that they even named a restaurant after it.

## 2. The Planetarium
The Planetarium is a great place to visit for people who are not of this world yet are too afraid to become an astronaut.

## 3. Armagh Food and Cider Festival
Every September the entire city goes into lockdown for the Armagh Food and Cider Festival. The shops get rid of all their stock and replace it with locally brewed cider. They hook everyone up to an IV drip and pump Linden Village straight into their veins. Despite its name, there's no food at this festival. There's just frozen blocks of cider that people shovel into their mouths to feel warm.

## 4. Road bowling
This is a tradition observed in the summer where local drunk farmers crowd around a lane in the back arse of nowhere and see who can throw a metallic ball the furthest. The person who can throw the ball down the road in the least amount of shots is declared the winner. The Armaghians are a people of great trust, they form a makeshift guard of honour around the contestant who is throwing, even though this steel object would definitely kill you if it hit you in the head.

## 5. Mumming
Mumming is a ritual as old as y'ArMagh herself. This is a tradition where the local Armaghians crowd together and drink Buckfast and then start wearing masks of bulls and horses. Mumming originates back in the period of Ancient Celtic Ireland. But now they're basically just furries.

**TOXICITY RATING: 7.8**

# Newry

Newry is a city in Armagh. Due to its proximity to the border, Newry is known as the Gateway to the North. But really, it's just a gateway to boredom. Or a fire escape from Dundalk at best. Citizens of Ireland come to Newry to escape from the tyrannical ways of minimum-unit alcohol pricing. Ever since then, the queues to get into the supermarket have been so long that many locals have starved to death waiting in line to get a loaf of Veda bread. It's believed the Newrians can spot the outsiders up here, because they're usually pushing a shopping trolley in each hand and have a heavy Dublin accent. Shopping trolleys are less respected than ever in Newry right now. A lot of them end up in the canal, which has become the eternal resting place of the shopping trolleys, where they rust in peace.

## Urban myths and legends

The spirit animal of Newrian consciousness is a chicken. A dead chicken. More specifically, a chicken fillet burger with coleslaw from Friar Tucks. The local Newrians flock around this chipper to douse themselves in greasy warmth. The homemade coleslaw in Friar Tucks ensures that no one from Newry will ever learn how to cook for themselves. Or chew with their mouth closed. Friar Tucks is an eco-friendly takeaway, it's fuelled entirely by the leg power of Marty Bogroll, Newry's most famous celebrity cyclist. Marty keeps the hopes and dreams of Newry in his majestic grey beard.

Another archetype of the Newry lifestyle is the local bus depot. The bus depot is a microcosm of Newrian existence. This is where the Hunger Games of Northern Ireland take place. In the bus depot, you'll find the first-year kids drinking cans of Boost and scoffing packets of Skips, while right next to them you'll find the 16-year-olds drinking Buckfast and smoking hash. To the left you'll spot the Newry Huns, not to be confused with the Newry Hens (which are currently hanging on a rack in Friar Tucks about to be stuck in the grill). The Newry Huns are a cohort of young females who have faded pink highlights in their hair, too many rings on their fingers and a broken phone speaker that they're playing tunes off of. It's often reported that if the first year accidentally inhales second-hand smoke, they will grow up to be like their older brother. Who's standing beside them at the bus depot, drinking Buckfast and smoking hash. The bus depot is basically an airport for people who aren't planning on setting foot in an airport for the next five years. The Newrian locals who brave the elements of this wretched bus depot eventually unify for a common purpose. They join together in their shared hatred of people from Warrenpoint.

## NIGHTLIFE

The Bank in Newry isn't really a bank. It's a financial institution of social capital. The Bank is the go-to spot for working professionals and millennials who like to pretend they have money. Due to the rates of inflation The Bank has grown expensive recently, but the little pods in the smoking area make you feel like you're living in a different universe: Fermanagh.

When visiting Newry make sure to pop into The Cobbles for a drink. If you'd like to observe a sample population of retired teachers in the local area, go here on a Thursday for karaoke night. You'll hear 'Dancing Queen' being butchered three times on the trot without anyone batting an eyelid.

Finally, be sure to sample the wares in Ginger Janes, a swanky new bar on Trevor Place. People were shocked when Ginger Janes burst onto the scene here and became a successful establishment, because in Newry, gingers aren't usually that popular.

Namaste.

## Armagh town

Armagh is the county town of County Armagh, because they didn't want to come up with another name. Armagh is perhaps the only entirely communist state in all of Europe. Not only do they believe in equal distribution of the wealth, they also share families, which is why Armagh is derived from 'our ma'.

## Urban myths and legends

The Slieve Gullion scenic drive is basically a giant forest that tourists trek to so they can look like they're in touch with nature. Not many people know that this turns into a casino at night time, but instead of playing blackjack people gamble with their lives by running through the forest and trying not to get attacked by the bears of Armagh. So far there have been zero casualties but that's not because bears don't exist here, it just means the Armaghians are really good at gambling.

Armagh is known as the oldest town in Ireland. Due to their lack of youth, Armagh tends to have amnesia. This leads to a very interesting game show the locals play called 'Who's Ma is it Anyway?' This is a quiz in which contestants compete to find out their ancestry but by the time they reach the commercial break they forget who they are and wonder why they're in the UK.

## NIGHTLIFE

Red Ned's is one of Armagh's favourite pubs. It caters to all needs. In fact, it has a massage table, a swimming pool, a helicopter landing pad, an organ from a church and a bowling alley. Here you'll find all walks of life and a vibrant atmosphere. An interesting thing happens in this pub. You can explore whatever section you like but you have to stay in your section. The bowlers can't talk to the lads watching the horse-racing. The organ player can't get a massage and has to face the wall. The helicopter pilot can't land before last orders and has to fly around Armagh pretending to have a purpose.

Everyone in Armagh loves going to the Armagh City Hotel the day after Christmas to an event known as 'The Bunker'. This is where all of Armagh comes together to rejoice in their festive spirit and equally distribute the Christmas presents amongst themselves. The Bunker is a good place to go if you want to experience how wonderful Armagh can be; but it's a bad place to go if you don't want to feel like you're on a crowded factory farm of drunken humans.

Namaste.

## Portadown

Portadown is a town in Armagh. It's also known as 'the hub of the North' just because they have a railway station that they won't stop talking about. Portadown is home to the Orange Order. A collection of men and women who are really into orange juice and even the occasional satsuma. Portadown is situated along the River Bann. Which is a river made entirely out of water, like most other rivers. This river winds all the way around Northern Ireland like a cold aquatic gown, before spitting in the mouth of the Atlantic Ocean.

### Urban myths and legends

It's believed that the nearby town of Lurgan was a social construction created by the people of Portadown just so they could spend the rest of eternity talking about how much they hate them. They decided to name it 'Lurgan' because Lurgan sounds like the name of grey porridge prison sludge.

There is a fantastic Lidl in the heart of Portadown and it's the pride and joy of the locals. They all genuflect at the altar beside the shopping trolleys, taking off their hats to take time out of their day, giving thanks to the gods of consumerism. And yes, in Portadown, they are all legally required to wear hats.

### Local cuisine

J.P.'s chipper is the crown jewel of the Portadownian lifestyle, famous for its humongous portions. It's rumoured that the fish and chips here are big enough to feed the entire town, with each family coming in in two-hour intervals to take their respective bites. J.P. is a local hero in Portadown. He goes to work in his pyjamas as a practical joke, just so he can say to people 'J.P.'s in his PJs' while smiling manically until they grab their chips and back away slowly. If you go to J.P.'s, make sure to try out their famous all-day breakfast, which is designed specifically for people who love eating breakfast for dinner, and despise natural sunlight.

## NIGHTLIFE

Bennett's is known to have the best pub food in all of Portadown. They have lovely pint sandwiches. The prices here are a little bit exclusive, in an effort to attract local middle-class lads who peaked in their college years. There's a lovely outdoor area in this pub that allows for a quiet, enjoyable drink to be peacefully consumed. Certain parameters have been set to ensure this standard is consistently met, including, but not limited to: the bouncers having a hidden machine that detects how loud everyone's voice is as they approach the bar. If it reaches above a certain decibel level, the bouncer pretends that there's no space inside and starts to awkwardly sing until the people trying to get into the bar back away.

Namaste.

# COUNTY CARLOW

Carlow in Irish means 'nothing to see here, drive on'. But the only problem with that is that there's so many roundabouts that you feel like you'll be here for the rest of your life. Carlow is in a state of turmoil; a war rages on between the Townies and the Burkes (the locals from Carlow town vs Graiguecullen). This apocalypse began back when Carlow disowned Graiguecullen and gave them to Laois. Because all that separates Graiguecullen from Carlow town is a bridge, chaos ensued.

# Top five things you don't want to miss:

**1. Watching people from Carlow IT trying to have a conversation with each other.**
This is a long-held tradition of the Carlow people. They say looking at two Carlow IT students trying to socialise with each other is as awkward as watching your parents having sex.

## 2. Doughnuts
Best experienced from the passenger side of a stolen car courtesy of a local joyrider.

## 3. Carlow pride
Experience the Carlow natives bragging about how great Carlow is as if they built the county themselves, despite there being nothing to do here.

## 4. Carlow County Museum
Much like number three in the list. Come to the Carlow County Museum to see a museum dedicated to everything that's ever happened in Carlow. It's about the size of your granny's shower.

## 5. Delta Sensory Gardens
Come here to see some of the nicest scenery in the entire country. Watch the flowers wither and die when a middle-aged man with a heavy Carlow accent gets too close to them.

**TOXICITY RATING: 9.1**

# Carlow town

Carlow town is the greatest place in Carlow. Most people from Carlow town haven't showered since the Normans invaded them in the twelfth century. Carlow town is an invigorating mixture of old and new. Which means it's a potent fusion of mainly two elements: drunk off-duty taxi drivers smoking Mayfairs squatting behind a bin singing Richie Kavanagh hits hoping to get a ten-minute segment on KCLR FM and Carlow IT college students getting into fights outside Supermac's.

## Urban myths and legends

The Carlow townians worship the Roadhouse Café. It's a mystical land where time seems to stand still, a phenomenon called Carlow time. The pubs and nightclubs of Carlow town love to treat this café as a sober house, sending their drunkest nightclub hopefuls to this eatery for sustenance before entering the club in a half hour. The cheese fries in the Roadhouse have magical healing properties, famous for sobering you up quicker than a line of cocaine. The Roadhouse is just Eddie Rocket's in a parallel dimension. A parallel dimension where everyone in Eddie Rocket's has a Carlow accent.

Carlow is famous for its water-based ceremonies. Every Carlow townian was baptised in the fountain. The fountain is a landmark of the town, and because Carlow is back to front, they don't call it a fountain, they call it 'the tree'. The locals conduct their ceremonial rituals by pushing the weakest member of each Carlow-based family into the fountain, which genetically shapes them to be afraid of water sports. The aquatic baptism also ingrains a magical force field in the locals that forbids them from ever leaving Carlow town, which is why everyone is stuck here, waiting to push the next vunerable member of Carlow society into their eventual demise.

The most interesting thing about Carlow town is rocks. Carlow has a massive rock called the Brownshill dolmen. It's the largest capstone in Europe, but deep down it's just a big stone. Some say the dolmen is a portal into Graiguecullen, an area that pretends to be in Laois, but is really just Carlow in disguise. Many rock enthusiasts have got sucked into the portal of Brownshill, only to land in Graiguecullen with no recollection of how they got there. Eventually leading to death by boredom.

## NIGHTLIFE

The Foundry is the inevitability of Carlowian nightlife. Everyone ends up in this nightclub on a night out. This isn't because they want to be here, it's just because the Foundry has magnets on the walls, and because everyone in Carlow is part-human part-faulty machine, the magnets inside their skin suck them into the Foundry whether they like it or not. Carlow townians like to claim that the Foundry is the biggest nightclub in the country. And to them, that's true. Because, as mentioned before, no one in Carlow town has ever experienced life outside Carlow. So to them, Carlow is an island.

Namaste.

# Graiguecullen

Graiguecullen is a small village in the countryside. No one really knows where it is, not even the people who live there. Graiguecullen is dangerously close to what can only be described as a cosmic wormhole: Carlow town. The other half of Graiguecullen is pretending to be in Laois. This haphazard existence on the border of a rock and a hard place has ingrained a deep sense of existential dread within the Graiguecullen natives. This eternal confusion echoes its way all through the surrounding areas.

## Urban myths and legends

Graiguecullen GAA club continues to rule over Graiguecullen with an iron fist. Because there's nothing else here. In fact, if you type 'Graiguecullen' into a Google search nothing shows up, just a Wikipedia page for the football team.

Graiguecullen suffers from a collective imposter syndrome of sorts. They just don't know who they're doing an impression of yet. The River Barrow is the dividing line of Graiguecullen. This river is what separates the townies from the countrysiders. No one knows which side is which, but they can't stop throwing rocks at each other. Despite this venomous raging civil war, no one has ever crossed the river, because people from

Graiguecullen don't know how to swim. Local property developers even built a swimming pool in the village as a cruel joke. As suspected, no one has ever been in the deep end without armbands.

Graiguecullen is a great place to hide things, due to its confusing geographical disposition. Most people just assume Graiguecullen is the name of an old Irish myth no one really cares about because it's not on TikTok. In fact, if you walk up to a local Graiguecullen youth and ask them what they know about the Croppies Grave down the road, the site where 600 Irish men were buried after an ambush in the 1798 rebellion, they'll just look at you and say 'you from Laois or Carlow pal?'

Both the Laois and Carlow county councils have been frantically trying to satiate the murderous palettes of the Graiguecullen locals. In an attempt to quell this civil unrest they decided to create Carlow Town Park as a peace offering to the Graiguecullen people. They took offence to this kind gesture, as Carlow Town Park used to be Carlow town dump, and after Graiguecullen had its way with it, it still is.

## Local ecosystem

The ecosystem of Graiguecullen is worth studying in itself. It's never dark here. Due to nobody knowing where Graiguecullen is, they're not under pressure to conform to the whims of the setting sun. As a result, it's daylight here 24/7. Allowing you to see people staring directly into the abyss, from everywhere you look.

Namaste.

# Tullow

Tullow is a market town in County Carlow. It is well served by two motorways, which is good news for visitors, as it makes Tullow really easy to escape from. Tullow is known as the granite town by the locals, because even they agree you would have to be constantly stoned to tolerate living in Carlow. Tullow is an ideal spot to stop in for a few days if you really want to go somewhere that will make you say 'Okay. I think I've seen enough.'

## Urban myths and legends

There's a statue of Father John Murphy in the Market Square. Father John Murphy was a political figure in the 1798 rebellion. Historians claim that Father John comes to life every night and starts sobbing hysterically about how no one knows who he is anymore, they just call him 'the statue' when he feels like he's so much more than that.

Famous Irish rugby player Seán O'Brien is the spiritual overlord of Tullow. His very existence has caused a dramatic shift in the Tullowian personality. Everyone in Tullow is infected by the Seán O'Brien pandemic. This is a condition known as SOBmosis: a disease characterised by acting like you know Seán O'Brien just because you're from Tullow and have literally nothing else interesting to talk about.

The Chocolate Garden of Ireland is a delicious business run by a family who own a forest full of chocolate trees in their garden. Some say the Chocolate Garden of Ireland is what you would get if you extradited Willy Wonka to life imprisonment in Carlow. The Chocolate Garden of Ireland hosts workshops on how to grow your own chocolate, and kids love it so much that they have often had to be pulled out of there with the jaws of life.

### NIGHTLIFE

JJ's is a cosy pub in the town. Reports suggest you might get so comfortable here that you have a nervous breakdown and think that this is your home. You finally snap out of it and come to your senses by realising that if this was your real home, you'd never let anyone play Irish country-rock music without kicking them out immediately.

Dalton's is another local favourite if you want to drink so much that you forget you're in Tullow. The staff in Dalton's are the next stage of human evolution. They have superhuman memory systems and will remember your drink of choice years after you entered their establishment.

The Tara Arms is a bar and grill often favoured by cyclists before they charter their hurried escape from Tullow. The Tara Arms is said to have the best carvery in all of Tullow. The Tara Arms used to have a full body, but then their sister pub, the Tara Legs, started kicking off. Now they are mutilated and the one arm doesn't know what the other leg is doing.

Namaste.

# COUNTY CAVAN

The county of Cavan is shaped like a chicken wing. But make sure not to tell the locals because they'll probably try to put it in a lunchbox and freeze it for when they get hungry again to save money on groceries. Cavan is known by the natives as 'Cyaaaaaavan'. No one knows how the extra 'y' got in there but all the additional letter a's were added because the locals thought if Cavan had extra letters, they could somehow get remunerated in tax-back. People from Cavan have computer brains. Everything has to make total logical sense or they will malfunction. There's no such thing as 'letting someone off' in Cavan. They will ask you for the 20 cent you owe them.

# Top five things you don't want to miss:

## 1. Sewage
Sewage is one of the favourite local pastimes here. Lay siege to your olfactory system in Cavan town. Inhale the sewage and see how the farmers live.

## 2. The 365 lakes
There are 365 lakes in Cavan, which make for stunning photos. Make sure to go early in the morning, to avoid the Cavan people who go there to wash their hair.

## 3. Walking everywhere
Walking is free, so people from Cavan love it.

## 4. Plateless dinners
Experience the local cuisine of Cavan. The locals are very conscious not to waste money on plates. They eat microwave meals directly out of their hands.

## 5. Cows
Cows. They are everywhere.

**TOXICITY RATING: 9.8**

# Ballinagh

Ballinagh is a remote village in the heart of Cavan. It's a sleepy enclave of small happenings, in fact, no one here ever leaves their home because they don't want to have anything to do with the outside world, which is how the area became known as 'Ballinah'. About two hundred years ago, Ballinagh was burnt to the ground because the government was worried it would become too interesting. Ironically, this great fire was the most interesting thing that ever happened in Ballinagh. Until it got burnt to the ground again about a hundred years later. It turns out people from Ballinagh really like playing with fire.

## Urban myths and legends

Killykeen Forest Park is a beautiful destination to go to if you love taking pictures of nature on Instagram to look like you aren't totally addicted to social media. Here you'll find many people who look like they're fishing. But if you look even closer, you'll see that I just made a typo, they're actually fisting. Fisting on a rowing boat surrounded by a body of water. Everyone in Ballinagh hates fish unless it's steak, which probably isn't fish anyway.

It's often been reported that locals of Ballinagh have been found to hang out in the Centra for every single waking moment of their lives. There is limited space in here, which causes a Battle Royale-style competition outside the shop every morning. Much like a breathless tyrant lugging onto the inhaler of the enemy so that their breath is another's breathlessness, the successors of this frantic frenzy are awarded a place in the shop so that they can hang out there all day and not be completely consumed with the boredom of living in Ballinagh.

The Ballinaghians have outgrown world religions and are now controlled by an even more powerful force: Kim Thanh, the local Chinese takeaway. Kim Thanh is an exclusive Chinese eatery that tries to throw people off the scent by having a name that sounds like a North Korean dictator. This name creates an air of exclusivity in the restaurant and only the bravest Ballinaghians will dare to trek to this magical place. The food in Kim Thanh is so good that it's never made anyone sick, but if it ever does, they'll have to change their name to Kim Thanh-ill.

## NIGHTLIFE

The Hatch is the preferred boozer of the Ballinagh natives. This hatch is home to excellent cheap pints of premium lager and has some of the best (and only) food in Ballinagh. They say the owner uses a water gun to shoot spring rolls in your uncle's mouth when your family gathers in the Hatch for your little cousins' christenings. The Hatch used to be called the Millennium, to try to convince the world that Cavan isn't living in the past, even though they were still showing ads on TV about how switching from punts to euros will be the way forward, up to a few weeks ago. The Millennium changed its name once the internet arrived in Ballinagh in 2019. Namaste.

## Cavan town

Yes, Cavan has a town in it. Years ago, the Cavan townsfolk got the nickname 'Cavanites'. This was due to what they have in common with stalactites. Because they both hang upside down for considerable periods of time and mostly live in caves. Cavan town, like most rural towns, is not a town. It just has a few shops and a post office. Public expenditure has zoned in on Cavan town, trying to pimp Cavan out to make it seem like a tourist trap. Which it is, but only because it traps tourists into inevitable disappointment.

### Urban myths and legends

The Cavanites worship the square in the town centre. This is where the locals pretend to relax and let loose. The residents of Cavan town are biologically encoded to love the square, due to its symmetrical shape. Instilling a sense of peace and purpose in the hearts and minds of the rigid and straight-laced Cavanites, who need everything to make logical sense.

It's believed the Cavanites are outrageously tight in every aspect of life. People from Cavan all share the same phone so they can save on buying their own credit. But because they're so stingy with money, they have no one to call. Everyone they love has been pushed away.

The sports shop in Cavan town has been standing there for six thousand years. Cavan town was never meant to be a town. The council just started building infrastructure around the sports shop and got carried away. Everyone in Cavan town and its environs has bought a county football jersey from the sports shop. When the jersey starts to stink, the locals just turn it inside out to save money on going to the laundrette.

## Local cuisine

When visiting Cavan town, make sure to stop for breakfast in the Hard Boiled Egg café. People from Cavan are only allowed eat their eggs hard-boiled, because it's the least emotional type of egg order, and because everyone in Cavan is aware of their emotional expenditure, they're only allowed cry approximately three times in their entire life. The Hard Boiled Egg café hosts the world's largest Irish breakfast challenge, consisting of ten sausages, ten rashers, ten eggs, five hash browns, five slices of white pudding, chips, three grilled tomatoes, mushrooms, a hill of beans and ten slices of toast. Everyone in Cavan town goes here once a week to compete in this challenge. They've realised that if they come here they don't need to eat for the rest of the week. Very few have ever won this competition, but you'll never hear from the ones that do, because they get put in the back of a van by men in black suits and have to live the rest of their days in a forest in Virginia under a new identity on a witness protection programme.

### NIGHTLIFE

The Farnham is one of the main nightclub destinations in Cavan town. This nightclub caters mainly to the type of people who would own a tractor licence and brag openly about it. Which is, basically everyone who has ever lived in Cavan.

The Imperial nightclub is Cavan's other den of Cavan-based activities. Since all of the nightclubs outside Cavan fell into extinction, the Imperial has become a melting pot for people from Leitrim, Fermanagh and Monaghan, along with other lads in double denim suits who wear brown shoes and know all the words to 'Sweet Caroline'.

Namaste.

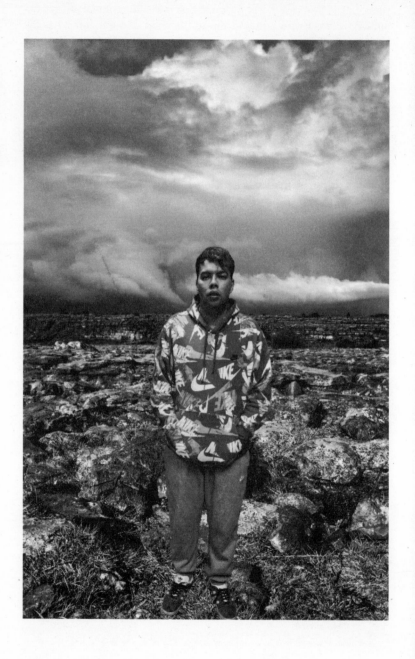

# COUNTY CLARE

Clare is known as the banner county. And the banner says *Get out while you can, or stay and bore yourself to death*. Some call Clare a blank canvas, because there is nothing to do here. The translation of Clare in Irish means a board or a plank, which perfectly describes the personalities of most of the people who live here. When dealing with someone from Clare, an unwritten rule of social etiquette states that if they even START to bring up the fact that the man who invented the submarine was from Clare, you're legally allowed to punch them in the throat without any repercussions.

# Top five things you don't want to miss:

## 1. The Burren

The Burren is a great place to visit if your life is such a mess that staring at rocks brings you joy. It's the perfect place to go for a scenic walk, especially if you want to twist your ankle on the uneven terrain. The Burren brings together a really specific breed of people. People who are interested in geology. Also known as an outdoor convention of the most boring people on earth.

## 2. The River Shannon

People from Clare are so pale they burn when they turn the radiator on. So to cool down, they jump into the River Shannon. Make sure to join them if you'd like to experience the plight of the locals. The course of the River Shannon is a metaphor for life in Clare, because no matter what you do, you inevitably end up in Limerick.

## 3. Destroying your tyres in a local pothole

Clare has some of the worst roads in the entire country. The county council could easily fix this but they are in bed with the local tyre-repair companies and love to see people get mad in public.

## 4. Playing the fiddle while getting chased around in a shopping trolley in Cloughleigh

This one is not to be missed, especially if you don't value life. This one is for the true adrenaline junkies who like to live on the edge. Get a local to push you around in a shopping trolley while you play the fiddle and hope that the angry mob don't catch up with you.

## 5. Going to Shannon airport and telling the US troops that 9/11 was an inside job

US troops are stationed at Shannon airport. Why not have fun with them?

**TOXICITY RATING: 8.3**

# Corofin

Corofin is a small village nestled in the bosom of Clare. It has often been known as the gateway to the Burren. Because the most interesting thing about this village is that it's a few miles away from a few big piles of rocks that people like taking pictures of. Corofin is a historical settlement and the village is dotted with ancient artefacts and prehistoric tombs. These tombs are known as wedge tombs. As you may suspect, wedge tombs are originally where wedges came from. True to the original recipe: the wedges here are stale and taste like rocks. The people from Corofin developed an evolutionary advantage by eating these wedge rocks. Now they have really sharp teeth and the most powerful bite in all of Clare and most of Limerick.

## What you'll find there

Corofin used to be one of the most powerful empires in all of Ireland until one day Brian Boru split it in half. He ordered that half of Corofin emigrate to Galway and the other half stay in Clare. This legend got handed down incorrectly over the years and now the people of Corofin are engaged in a civil war against the Corofinnians in Galway. They think they just happened to both be called Corofin. Some day we can hope for the reunification of the two Corofin states. A region rebuilt and moving towards a brighter future. But for now, they will continue to shoot fireworks at each other and rob the WiFi in Ennis to join each other's local Facebook community pages and unleash hurtful remarks and violent tirades upon each other.

Corofin is a postmodern metaphorical protest against the monopoly of Airbnb. The bed-and-breakfast industry is booming here. There are seventeen million B&Bs in the small village but most of them are so quaint that you can't even see them. Corofin is a stronghold against technological advancement. Everyone here still gets the weather forecast on teletext.

Make sure to visit the Festival of Finn that takes place here every year. This festival is famous not only for its stone-throwing competitions and Ireland's greatest beard and moustache championship, but also for the less popular third competition, which is a combination of the first two. Throwing rocks at lads who grew facial hair all year for local recognition.

## NIGHTLIFE

Nobody knows this, but if you go to the Burren at 3 a.m. it will be dark. If you kick a pile of rocks in the shape of a Celtic cross a magical portal will open up and transport you into an American fast-food diner. This is a diner like no other, it doesn't serve food. It's food forward, so you have to take your clothes off and lie down on a plate and let the food judge you. It turns out this mythical diner is actually in the other Corofin and every time someone falls into the portal, Corofin vs Corofin relations improve in a really insignificant way.

Namaste.

# Ennis

Clare went through its own version of the enlightenment era; it involved figuring out how to use a microwave, a feat no one from Clare has ever been able to achieve before. Out of this revelation, Ennis awoke. With an unmerciful hangover.

Ennis is the county town of Clare. It's a sprawling urban centre situated along the River Fergus. They say if you walk towards the river at night time Fergus himself will jump out of the bush and try to have a deep meaningful conversation with you. Ennis is powered entirely by the vol-au-vents in the Old Ground Hotel, a rite of passage for every hungry Ennis native who's too cheap to rent a room for the night.

## Urban myths and legends

The pathways of Ennis are so narrow that if you walk by someone you're forced to talk to them. This is why Ennis is known as the friendliest town in Ireland. It's not because they're nice people, it's because they don't have a choice. The architecture is making them do it.

Ennis is a black hole that keeps people there for centuries. The only time anyone leaves Ennis is to go to college. They inevitably find themselves coming back due to the inescapable quality of the battered sausage in Fat Chip Enzo's. Many young people drop out of their philosophy degree in UL just to eat a garlic cheese chips out of a silver tray like a farmyard animal.

Some of the population fondly refer to Ennis as 'E-town', even going so far as to get a tattoo on their back that says 'E-town 'til I die' or 'E-town on top'. These people are known as E-heads. In other words, they're lads who go around the town in a Honda Civic slinging one-gram twenty-five bags while blaring DMX on their speaker. The E-heads feel a connection with DMX. It's not because they can rap. They just like DXM, but they're dyslexic and think it's the same thing.

### *NIGHTLIFE*

There's an unwritten rule in Ennis that you can only marry someone if they also happen to be from Ennis. All of these marriages began in Queens Hotel nightclub. A nightclub as old as the Queen herself. This was where many of the children of Ennis were conceived. Often to the background noise of 'Maniac 2000'. There are five bars in the Queens nightclub. One for every day of the week.

Namaste.

# COUNTY CORK

People from Cork always sound like they have food in their mouth. And they usually do. Their lack of self-consciousness makes them speak with their mouth full. Usually at a deafening volume. Corkonians never specify whereabouts in Cork they're from. This is known as Cork collectivism. They all just say they're from Cork. Unless it's West Cork, which is a different continent entirely. Corkians are so brainwashed by Cork that they see the need to bring Cork into everything they do. But they usually don't do much other than tell everyone within earshot that they're from Cork.

# Top five things you don't want to miss:

## 1. Hearing a local call Cork the real capital
This is the most popular form of entertainment in Cork. It's guaranteed a laugh every time. If Ireland is the single parent and Cork and Dublin are brothers, Dublin gets to smoke Amber Leaf in his room while Cork gets in trouble for having a smell of cider on his breath after going to see The Coronas in the Marquee.

## 2. A trip to the English Market
This is a great place to visit, even if the title is a bit misleading. You can't actually buy English people here. Just people from West Cork, which is almost the same thing; people from West Cork are basically English people with more money, even though it seems like they never work. Probably because they're always getting kidnapped and brought down to the English Market.

## 3. Facing your fear of heights on top of the Shandon Bells
The Shandon Bells is one of the tallest buildings in Cork. A terrifying place for people who feel like their soul will leave their body whenever they find themselves on an elevated surface. Rise up! Let's get close to Jesus!

## 4. Spike Island
Spike Island used to be a prison in Cork. Now it's a museum. Spike Island got its name for being full of pricks.

## 5. Looking for Roy Keane and asking him to give you your football back
Do this at your own peril. Roy Keane doesn't believe in private ownership of property. But if you love getting into fights, walk up to Roy and say 'it's my ball I'm going home'.

**TOXICITY RATING: 8.2**

# Cork City

Cork City is often referred to as the real capital of Ireland to make them feel better about their accent. An accent which often gets mistaken for the sound of a crow gasping for life. Corkonians say 'like' at the end of a sentence for no reason. If you took all the likes out of a Cork person's mouth and had to put them all in the same place, they'd barely fit in Páirc Uí Chaoimh. Everyone in Cork frequently says 'JU KNOW WHATT' as if they're about to say something really deep, but they never do. Corkonians all talk in block capitals. Cork are also known as the rebels but the only rebel they had was Michael Collins and they shot him.

No one in Cork can remember anyone's name, which is why Corkonians are either called bai, kid or girl. They're too consumed with Cork-related imagery to live in the present moment. They just have too much Cork in them. This is known as Cork-centrism. In Cork you're either a langer or you're langers. A langer is a Cork native, and langers is a drunk Cork native, which is usually . . . most of them. All the time.

Cork see themselves as their own country, the Texas of Ireland. Cork chose to vote against the euro at the turn of the millennium. Many who went down to Cork for a weekend away are still stuck there with nowhere to go because they forgot to change their euros into punts.

Everyone from Cork City has the personality of someone with an unironic mullet.

## Urban myths and legends

St Patrick's Street is the commercial epicentre of Cork City. The locals fondly call Patrick Street 'Pana' because people from Cork don't like using long words. At the end of Patrick Street you'll find a statue of Fr Matthew, a Cork man who led the temperance movement in the 1800s. The only reason people in Cork don't get upset at this statue is because no one in Cork knows what the temperance movement is.

The North and Southside divide has been a plague to the Corkian ecosystem for centuries. Whenever the Northsiders can get the busfare together, they make their way into the city to ruin everyone's night. The Mayfield-Montenotte power struggle has been the Northside's dark secret since time began. Everyone from Mayfield says they're from Montenotte but no one believes them, and everyone from Montenotte, due to a pang of social class guilt, likes to play down their privilege and claim to be from Mayfield. They give themselves away because they have a slightly more nasal accent than the rest of the Cork natives, this is locally known as 'Snotty Montenotte.'

South Mall is the central business district of Cork City but the businesses are only allowed use Monopoly money and loose fivers. If a non-Cork business tries to set up shop in South Mall all the Corkonian business owners crowd around them and squawk until the invaders can't take it anymore and move to Limerick.

Cork City used to be a swamp, and it still is. Roy Keane is king of the swamp.

The Butter Museum is a notorious hotspot for people who are weirdly obsessed with butter. Everyone in the Butter Museum has a relatively similar experience. Usually something along the lines of 'What am I doing in Cork? Why am I at a museum made out of butter? And can someone please tell me, why I have an erection?'

The Cork Opera House is where Corkonians go to sing, and due to their unusual accents, all someone from Cork has to do to sing is open their mouth and drag out their words slightly more than they already do.

The main attraction of Plunkett Street is the *Echo* man, who sells the *Evening Echo* newspaper and screams '*Echo Echo Echo!*' The *Echo* man is a simulation and can only be heard by Cork people, as they needed a distraction from focusing all their energy on hating people from Dublin.

Everyone from Cork thinks West Cork is another universe, because people from West Cork have fake British accents due to them having to mould their personality to make them appropriate for tourist consumption in another country, so people from Cork City go on their holidays to West Cork and act like they're in Spain. When you close your eyes, Kinsale does look a bit like Marbella, in fairness. No one from West Cork has ever successfully travelled all the way to Cork City because once they enter Cork itself, they'd never find their way home. It's far too confusing, there's just too many bridges.

## Mallow

Mallow is a town nestled in the suburbs of Cork. Built on the River Blackwater, it used to be a defensive settlement. Now it's a self-contained isolation unit full of defensive Mallow heads who refuse to go to Cork City because they believe it doesn't exist. Everyone from Mallow thinks Mallow is the capital of Cork.

Due to unseen forces at work that keep Mallow in a state of perpetual fear, no one from Mallow has ever been outside Mallow. All the locals are implanted with ankle bracelets so the powers-that-be know their exact whereabouts at all times. The power that controls Mallow is known as the Mallow Maintenance Programme (MMP). They have placed back-scratchers in all the houses of Mallow, which is why everyone from Mallow has scratches all over their body. The MMP is run by a group of failed TDs who would never get elected due to their militant Mallow beliefs. This MMP is the reason why, whenever a local travels past the roundabout on the Limerick road out of Mallow, they have a panic attack. The MMP also controls the weather, which is why it never rains. Although, due to its proximity to the river, it does flood once a year. Thankfully, this doesn't disrupt the life in Mallow too much, because everyone in Mallow is waterproof.

## Urban myths and legends

Mallow entices tourists to enter its inescapable realm using the magical forces of Mallow Castle. Once the Irish-American holiday-goers enter the grounds, the gates close behind them and they're forced to work on the land until they develop a thick Cork accent. Any tourists that resist get turned into a donkey and have to spend the rest of their days in the donkey sanctuary down the road.

There is a rest and relaxation room in Mallow called the MarshMallow. As you can imagine, it's a gigantic room with a host of giant marshmallows to sleep on. As soon as you're about to drift out of consciousness a man in a lab coat comes up to you and asks you what your relationship with your parents is like. This man forces you into a deep meaningful conversation and won't leave until you cry. This is part of the MMP's devious plan to break the spirit of the Mallow natives so that they never try to leave.

### NIGHTLIFE

The Hawks Bar is an intricate ecosystem where famous actors go to get hammered and drink other people's pints when they're not looking. Mallow also has a nightclub known as Chasers. This is the only late bar in Mallow and it got its name because anyone from Cork City who tried to get in got chased out with a cattle prod. This is where the humans of Mallow socially interface with each other. Usually saying something like 'well bai' or 'well girl', before dancing and grunting to themselves. If you ever get barred from Chasers, there's nowhere else to go. It's reported a chemical reaction occurs once the bouncers throw you out. You immediately become sixty-five years old and wear a farmer's cap and nothing else. Namaste.

# Youghal

Youghal is a seaside resort town in the east of County Cork. This is the nesting place of the Norries (people from the northside of Cork). The Norries congregate here every summer to sit down in a pub beside the beach staring at a picture of the sun for fifteen-minute intervals before taking a break. Because Norries can only stare at a picture of the sun in short bursts before getting sunstroke.

## What you'll find here

Youghal is a treasure trove of good times for Cork-based holiday-goers who are too stubborn to make the descent all the way down to West Cork. There are more beaches in Youghal than there are statues of Eddie Hobbs. Although, there are no statues of Eddie Hobbs here. The beaches are some of the most beautiful in the country and during the summer months everyone in Youghal shrinks down to a miniscule level and Eddie Hobbs makes sandcastles for all the locals to live in.

The Regal Cinema is a posh cinema that doubles as a wine bar, basically the opposite of a beach. If you go here in a Cork jersey the security guard will assume you've never been invited to the Cannes film festival and will point you to a nearby director who will make a patronising biopic about growing up in a Cork that's developing too fast for a down-to-earth middle-aged man in his twenties to keep up with.

Overlooking the town of Youghal is the famous clocktower. It's the biggest skyscraper in the area and if you get to the top you can see the entire town. People often report feelings of shock when looking down. Usually saying things like 'I feel sick, why are we in Youghal?' There's a secret shopping centre on the top of the clock tower that only opens when everyone is asleep. It's known as the Mall of Youghal and it's run by really tired werewolves.

## Bantry

Bantry is a world-renowned tourist destination, famous for being the home of Irish people with fake English accents. Everyone in Bantry is a descendant of Oliver Cromwell. They caught the OliCrom variant and now they can't stop thinking about the Queen. Everyone who lives in Bantry is a landlord, they have fever dreams of turning the rolling hills of Bantry into a giant golf course. Bantry is dotted with lighthouses. If you took an aerial photograph of Bantry at night it would look like a massive rave, or the inside of a dentist's mouth whose teeth are falling out because he keeps getting into fights on the weekend. When sitting on the mountains in Bantry on a clear day, you feel at peace knowing that the Instagram post you make about your stay in West Cork is going to make your friends that hate you think you have your life together. You don't.

### Urban myths and legends

At the bottom of Bantry Bay lies a peninsula called Sheep's Head. This is where the natives go to sacrifice animals. The people of Bantry Bay host a ceremony every Halloween at Sheep's Head where they sing the British national anthem and barbeque a rack of lamb. To the uninitiated observer, it might seem like the costumes they wear are a bit over the top, but really they're just Bantry locals in sheep's clothing.

Unlike in Dublin, wild horses roaming around in the fields of Bantry are actually a sign of wealth and prosperity. Bantry is so economically developed that they call horse-riding 'equestrian activities'. Bantry stands out from the rest of West Cork because everyone who lives in Bantry was a horse in a previous life, which means all the horses in Bantry are just future Bantry humans. My theory about the horse-human evolution of Bantry can be easily proven. Everyone in Bantry has a ponytail and they love when you pull it. They're also secretly addicted to ketamine and sleep on bales of hay.

Bantry is a haven for kayak enthusiasts and other annoying families that think it's fun to do things outdoors. Every tourist that comes to Bantry has never actually set foot indoors. They all shit in a bush and eat leaves.

## NIGHTLIFE

Ma Murphy's is the most famous pub in Bantry. It has a hollowed-out shop front at the entrance with a bar out the back. No one knows who Murphy's Ma is. But rumour has it that she was the shopkeeper who owned the building out the front. One day she told Murphy she was going out to the shop for cigarettes. Murphy knew she was lying because she lived in a shop, didn't smoke and never came back. Murphy was left to fend for himself and built this really popular traditional Irish pub in case his Mam ever decided she got bored of abandoning him and came back. She didn't.

Cargo nightclub is the only club in Bantry. It contains a strict dress code of Ben Sherman T-shirts, jeans and those black non-slip shoes you get in Dunnes Stores. It's believed every time the DJ here plays 'Paradise' by George Ezra and three generations of the same family get up to dance, it creates a fracture in the bottom of the seabed that will eventually rise up through the calming currents of Bantry Beach onto the harbour and swallow up a surfer who's trying to make a TikTok video on his board while obsessing over his hair. It's believed the surfers of Bantry all get placed into a surfer jail where they get their surfboards and smartphones taken off them and every time they talk about themselves they get electrocuted with a shock collar.

Namaste.

# Mahon

Mahon is a residential suburb in Cork City. Some say Mahon is the Blanchardstown of Cork, because if they took away the shopping centre, there would be nothing left. Most of the famous tourist destinations in Mahon are in the neighbouring village of Blackrock, the affluent suburb that Mahonians pretend to be from when they want to get into any night-club in the city. Blackrock natives only ever go to Mahon to buy designer clothes, they think Mahon is only a shopping centre. Because people from Blackrock are used to the luxurious lifestyle, they never see the struggle, all they see are opportunities for growth.

## Urban myths and legends

Mahon Point shopping mall is an airport that doesn't go anywhere. This labyrinth of consumerism has a strict code of ethics that only allows Cork City-related media into the area. This is why most of the shops here are closed, but the ones that are open only sell Cork City FC jerseys. Dunnes Stores was founded by Ben Dunne, originally from Mahon. Ben wanted to show his county pride by making sure everything in this shopping centre had something to do with Cork. Even the cinema in here shows edited clips of Roy Keane shouting on a panel show for three hours at a time.

When visiting Mahon, make sure to take a brisk walk along the peninsula. Depending on what time of the day you go there, anywhere from brisk walk to running for your life will do just fine. That's because no matter when you visit the peninsula there's always a 63 per cent chance of getting run over by a raging cyclist. These impatient pedallers have been cast to the purgatory of the peninsula to take part in a game to see how many innocent civilians they can injure. If you survive this expedition, you'll have made it to the end of the harbour, where you'll see ships stand so high they block out the light of the sun, which is why no one in Mahon ever gets a tan.

Everyone in Mahon worships the idol of the area, Derek. Derek owns a corner shop called Meadowgrove Stores, but everyone just calls it Derek's shop because it's easier to remember. Derek's shop is Mahon's very own slice of Narnia. No one in Mahon ever needs to venture into Blackrock because Derek has something for everyone. The shop stretches so far back that some locals are still trying to find their way out, navigating a route through all of the unavoidable bargains.

## Clonakilty

Clonakilty is a busy market town in the heart of West Cork. Some call it a metropolitan hub of Irish tourism. Even though the word metropolitan comes from the word 'metropole', which means the parent nation of a colony. Which explains why everyone here has a fake British accent and calls Boris Johnson 'Daddy'. Clonakilty has several quaint artisanal coffee shops. Great places to go if you like pretending to enjoy homegrown blueberry jam that a West Cork landlord grew in their tenant's bath. Everyone in West Cork is a landlord. Even if they don't own a property, landlordism is a state of mind, and to them, it comes naturally.

### What you'll find here

Clonakilty is the home of black pudding. This is the main draw of Clonakilty. They're famous for being responsible for the part of my breakfast I always leave on my plate because I hate it. Thanks Clonakilty! Due to black pudding being such a major export on the world stage of consumerism, the people of Clonakilty have developed a non-offensive, non-specific persona of what way they think tourists want them to be. Clonakiltians are a mirror of tourist fetishism. They eat black pudding 24/7 and cry themselves to sleep because they secretly want to eat Coco Pops.

Everyone in Clonakilty loves surfing, but nobody can swim. In stormy weather, the people of Clonakilty gather on the beach to bet on who's going to drown next. Clonakilty has a Friday market where rich farmers magically appear out of nowhere to peddle their wares, offering their organic local produce to open-mouthed tourists. It's reported that when natives from Cork City go here on their summer holidays, it is common for them to accidentally consume small-batch vegan chocolates. This confuses their unaccustomed taste buds so much that it kills them on the spot.

When visiting Clonakilty, make sure to pop into one of the many colourful boutique shops with their even more colourful owners. It's believed there are some shopkeepers here who might get you to join the Cult of West Cork (COWC). If you agree to joining their cult, they will whisk you away into a dark room and force you to watch propaganda videos about the Queen as well as embedding you with neuro-linguistic programming that makes you call West Cork West Britain.

## NIGHTLIFE

Due to the constant pressure of tourist expectations, no one in Clonakilty knows how to relax. But if you want to see the locals pretend to chill out, try out Teach Beag, which is a cute cottage that serves alcohol. Teach Beag in English means 'little house' and it's the only little house in Clonakilty. Here you can see Clonakiltians pretend to get drunk on Guinness and have a great time. It's so convincing that you might start enjoying yourself too.

Namaste.

# COUNTY DERRY

Derry is also known as Londonderry. But I've been told by a local that the first six letters are just there for decoration, not meant to be pronounced.

## Top five things you don't want to miss:

### 1. The murals
Or more specifically, walking up to the murals of Irish freedom fighters and asking the nearest person if these paintings are characters in *Derry Girls*.

### 2. Taking a trip to South Derry
They say to start a rave here all you have to do is throw a football in the air and watch the locals fight for their lives.

### 3. Taking a trip to North Derry
They say to start a rave here all you have to do is throw an English muffin in the air and watch the locals fight for their lives.

### 4. Playing hide-and-seek with Martin O'Neill
Everyone knows that Martin O'Neill lives under the peace bridge. He got exiled to a life under the bridge when he lost in a dancing competition against Steve Staunton. Now Martin is court-ordered to play hide-and-seek with anyone who requests it of him. Martin is competitive. He won't let you win. But if you do, he will rage-cry and scream so loud it will push the peace process back by another five years.

### 5. Trying to climb up the walls in the city with Dana pulling you down by the leg
Nobody knows where Dana came from, but we think she was hiding behind one of those bins waiting for the next potential wall-hopper. Dana believes in equality of opportunity, she will pull anyone's leg to keep them in Derry for as long as possible.

**TOXICITY RATING: 6.4**

# Coleraine

Coleraine is a market town in Derry. But it's also named after a drug called Coleraine. Coleraine is a bit like cocaine but when you sniff a line, instead of euphoria, it makes the world grey.

Coleraine is the Navan of Northern Ireland, because everything here is in sepia-tone and makes you want to run for your life. The people of Coleraine spend most of their lives talking about how they want to move to a far-away, exotic land some day, but they're really just talking about Belfast. Which is lightyears away for most sleepy Colerainians, they usually never make it past Portrush. The Coleraine natives have to wear an item of clothing called the coleraine collar. It's an electrical instrument they wear around their neck and if they stray too far away from the homeland they get zapped.

Coleraine suffers from a palpable sadness because most people who travel through this region are transient. They never stay. They're just stopping off here from Dublin on the way to Belfast to buy fireworks. This makes the locals look like they're crying, but because Colerainians had to detach from their emotions at an early age to save themselves from a lifetime of boredom, the tears are purely a physiological response. This is a facial stress reaction known as Coleraining.

## What you'll find here

Coleraine is a great holiday destination if you want your holiday to consist of exploring different coffee shops and charity stores, because in Coleraine there's literally nothing else to do. Some people say Coleraine is boring, but I say no no no! Coleraine isn't boring, Coleraine is a social experiment that the government conducted to see what would happen if they shut down everything that could ever be deemed as mildly interesting to anyone, ever.

The only relic of commercialism that survived in the communist state of Coleraine is the Jet Centre. The Jet Centre is a massive arcade and bowling alley. Unfortunately, there are no jets in the Jet Centre, which means that as much as you may wish to be fired out of Coleraine in a rocket, it'll never happen. The natives of Coleraine don't believe in aircraft travel. It goes against their religious beliefs.

## Local cuisine

Whenever they're not rolling around in a wet patch of muck looking at the clouds go by, sometimes Colerainians like to eat. No one from Coleraine ever learned how to cook due to the consistent temptation of Sun Do, a local Chinese takeaway seducing the locals into a silver tray of satay chicken. Sun Do is actually a living organism. It's Sun Do during the day and at night time it's Sun Don't, a classic 1950s American diner. But because no one in Coleraine is allowed out of their homes after 6 p.m., no one will ever know the truth.

Namaste.

# Derry City

Derry is a city in the heart of County Derry, obviously. Derry is often overlooked because the walls surrounding its borders make outsiders climb up and take a curious peek. But Derry is mostly overlooked because it's not Belfast. You can take a walk along the walls of the city for a picturesque view of Derry's architecture. There are cannons dotted along the walls, reminding you that it's important not to get too relaxed here. Derry suffers from an identity crisis. Some people aren't sure whether to call the area Derry or Londonderry. It's not that difficult. People who call Derry Londonderry think Derry is in London, and others have been spray-painting walls saying 'Free Derry' because they thought the milkman would give them free bottles of milk imported from the South. To avoid confrontation, Derry is Londonderry from Monday to Thursday and Derry is Derry on the weekends.

## What you'll find here

Just outside the city walls lies Guildhall. Guildhall is a famous tourist attraction in Derry. It's basically a coffee shop with nice windows. The clocktower in the Guildhall was modelled as the IKEA version of Big Ben. This made it a target for bombings during the troubles. Because the IRA hate IKEA. If there's one thing that the IRA despise, it's sharing their vowels with homeware stores.

When visiting Derry, make sure to make a pit stop at the peace bridge. The peace bridge in the city centre was erected in 2011, it's the place where cyclists and pedestrians merge as one. When walking along the peace bridge, the flurry of fast-paced bikes zooming right past and almost impaling you combined with trying to hopscotch along the path to avoid the dog shit makes the peace bridge the least peaceful place in Derry.

The ancient battle between the bogside and the waterside rages on through the heart of Derry. The bogside have *Derry Girls* and the waterside have the UVF. Someone in the bogside painted a mural of the Derry Girls over the murals of civil rights leaders. This means that the only way *Derry Girls* can Free Derry once and for all is by getting into a game of naked twister with a group of Loyalist paramilitaries.

Seamus Heaney is the spiritual leader of Derry. Heaney inspired generations of Derry locals. Just because he could write poetry, now all the kids in Derry think they can rap. But everyone knows the only good rappers in Derry are Kneecap. And they're from Belfast.

## NIGHTLIFE

Sandinos is the place to go if you'd like to see hipsters socialise with each other. There are so many different pale ales in here that some of them haven't even been invented yet. Sandinos has a split personality. Downstairs, a quaint pub with friendly locals; upstairs, a nightclub of college students accidentally spilling drinks on each other. Sandinos is a great pub to go to if you like standing up all night. There are so many people here that you'd have a better chance getting a seat on the *Titanic*.

Namaste.

# COUNTY DONEGAL

Everyone thinks people from Donegal are nice just because of their soft-spoken accent. If you were approached by an axe-wielding psychopath from Donegal you'd never be able to take them seriously because they sound so relaxed. No one from Donegal has ever raised their voice, which is absolutely terrifying. Donegal is situated right beside Derry. But the North didn't want Donegal because they thought it would make the monarchy look less intimidating.

# Top five things you don't want to miss:

## 1. Twin-cams

Twin-cams are the national motor of Donegal. Observe the car enthusiasts of Letterkenny in their natural habitat, doing laps around the town all night looking for an open space to drop a gear and let it rip. You can also find them listening to DJ Cammy shouting at people out the window like it's 2006. The car enthusiasts are legally not allowed call themselves boy racers because many of them are well into their late 30s and often have a bench warrant for reckless driving and a restraining order from their ex.

## 2. Going to the beach in Bundoran and trying not to fall down the hill and smash your face off a rock

It was my first ever holiday. I went to Bundoran and fell down the hill and smashed my face off a rock. There was so much blood.

## 3. Telling a lad from Donegal that you thought he was Scottish

It's not ignorant to mix them up. It's not your fault they have weird accents. Donegal, please do better.

## 4. Asking a local if Donegal is in Northern Ireland and then running for your life

You'll see the tears well up in their eyes before they rev up the engine and try to hit you with their car.

## 5. The Donegal Squat

The Donegal Squat is a squat specific to Donegal. It consists of bending down, keeping your back straight and picking up a cigarette butt directly off the ground, lighting it and smoking it in front of horrified onlookers.

**TOXICITY RATING: 7.8**

# Bundoran

Bundoran is an idyllic seaside town on the west coast of Donegal. It's also known as the IRA's jacuzzi due to the fact that so many Irish Republicans come down here to go to a health and wellness clinic to have their backs waxed.

## What you'll find here

In the summertime thousands of empty-headed vessels flock to Bundoran to destroy it. Bundoran is a whore of Irish tourism. This town relies entirely on Americans dropping ice-cream cones on the ground and not picking up after themselves. As well as lads who travelled up from Westmeath getting sick in the bin because they are trying to find the sweet spot between having a good time and death by alcohol poisoning.

Bundoran is overrun by drunk middle-aged men and women from Carlow with really loud voices every year for Sea Sessions, Bundoran's annual music festival,which has previously featured acts such as Dizzee Rascal, The Sugarhill Gang and Two Door Cinema Club. It's believed there's no music at the festival, they just lock those three acts in a room with each other and don't let them out til they gained acceptance over the fact that the promoter duped them into coming here by telling them it was Electric Picnic. Unfortunately, this happy day never arrived and they all died.

Bundoran is a microcosm for life itself, if life itself consisted purely of Irish Republicans and kite-surfing hippies who use words like 'choppy' far too casually in a sentence. The hipsters of Ulster can also be found flocking to Bundoran. That's why there is an overload of over-priced specialty coffee outlets, craft-beer breweries and middle-aged men with handlebar moustaches weeping into their spoken-word poetry journals.

All these personality types battle for dominance in the coliseum of Bundoran: Bundoran Adventure Park. While this park may pose as a theme park, it's really an arena of war and destruction. The hipsters, hippies and Republicans engage in devastating battle, although the hippies and hipsters form an allegiance after realising they have a lot in common. Most of them end up in a field somewhere drinking kombucha, leaving the rest of their people defenceless. The Republicans always win eventually.

Namaste.

# Letterkenny

Letterkenny is the biggest town in County Donegal. It is often referred to as 'the gateway to the South' by Republican pint-drinking men. The Unionists tend to not even be aware of its existence, usually the same people who think the Fleadh Cheoil is a type of insect that only stings people who are obsessed with Irish culture.

## What you'll find here

Letterkenny is flooded for a weekend every summer with boy racers from every corner of the universe, a pilgrimage of parka-jacket-wearing youths who puff pre-rolled cigarettes dangerously close to a petrol tank. This ritual is known as the Donegal Car Rally. Despite its name, no one ever really watches the rally, they just hang around outside their dad's Subaru and drink cheap cans of cider, listening to '90s dance tunes on someone's Spotify playlist on a half-broken speaker they bought on Wish.com until the ads come on because they didn't pay for premium. At which point they are excommunicated from this cult and have to use a bicycle to get to their next destination: endless laps around the town for the rest of eternity.

The LYIT is the local third-level college in Letterkenny. This is an interesting multi-purpose facility, where young adults of the North-West flock to study computers for a year, at which point, the second year of the course in LYIT offers a fire exit and an introduction into a career of construction work or makeup tutorials.

Every bank holiday weekend Letterkenny becomes a bottleneck, jammed with Northern Irish holiday-goers. The legend goes that the Northerners actually suffer from partial blindness and deafness, because when they enter Letterkenny, it's as if they don't see or hear the locals. This great blind spot makes it so that in their eyes, the people of Letterkenny don't even exist. The Northern Irish have no need to engage with the natives anyway, seeing as they always bring their own food and drink down.

Letterkenny natives communicate through edible symbols, which signify social meaning. This meaning is constructed in the Four Lanterns chipper, a Mecca of fast-food culture. The Letterkenny natives eat garlic cheese chips for breakfast, lunch and dinner. It's the only suitable food source in the entire Donegalian universe.

## *NIGHTLIFE*

The Pulse Nightclub is the famous hotspot of social drinkers in the Letterkennian ecosystem. It's a great place to go if you want to jump on anything with a heartbeat, which is actually where it got its name from. The Pulse is the place to be if you want to listen to a mash-up of country and pop music. It's alleged that there is a gigantic cow's heart in the middle of the dance floor. It's believed that everyone worships this cow's heart and touches it for eternal life. These reports can not be confirmed or denied at this time.

Namaste.

# COUNTY DOWN

County Down is a county at the top of the Island of Ireland, so really it should be called County Up. But the natives of Down look at everything backwards because their compasses are broken and they think they're part of the UK. County Down is like vanilla ice cream. Good when mixed with other stuff but by itself it's no match for the Protestants. If you are Down for long enough it might turn into a depressive episode. Down is upset because they only have half of Belfast and half of Newry and Lisburn. The government know Down would be far too happy if they were allowed to be a sovereign state.

# Top five things you don't want to miss:

## 1. Telling a local you were up in Down

They've definitely never heard anyone say that before. Watch the reaction of a local as you make a pun about the name of their county to witness the true desperation of life in a county that has nothing in it. Watch them squirm as they try to make a comeback and start stuttering.

## 2. Stopping one of the locals waiting at a bus stop and asking them to help you find St Patrick

St Patrick was buried here somewhere. Scare one of the locals into helping you find him for once and for all.

## 3. Going to Warrenpoint and asking someone for a lend of a tenner

They will definitely have it. Everyone in Warrenpoint is rich. Which is why they will definitely not give it to you.

## 4. Burr Point

Go to Burr Point in Down. It's Ireland's most easterly point. The perfect place to go if you want to feel the experience of being as close to Russia as possible without having to go to Cork.

## 5. Tollymore Forest Park

Take a walk around Tollymore Forest Park and shout at one of those really irritating families that love being in nature. Ask why they don't just watch Netflix on the weekends like normal people.

**TOXICITY RATING: 7.9**

# Portaferry

Portaferry is a small village on the coast of County Down. Portaferry is often confused with Portadown, Portrane, Portstewart and the neighbouring area of Portavogie. Portaferry is one of the island's hidden gems and they chose their name to try to throw you off ever coming here. With so many places in the North starting with 'Porta—' you won't be bothered scrolling all the way down on Google Maps to find it.

## Urban myths and legends

The children of Portaferry love the rain. Because in torrential weather, the ferry is cancelled, meaning they can't go to school. Despite this, the government of Portaferry refuse to build a school, because they think getting a ferry every day and praying it doesn't show up is great for personal development. This strange glitch in Portaferrian consciousness has evolved to follow these children into adulthood. These former children all still worship the rain as a result of their upbringing. The sunniest place they'll ever go is Donegal. Once it goes above 20 degrees Celsius, they burst into tears.

## What you'll find here

Portaferry overlooks Strangford Lough. This is the main tourist attraction of the area. A haven for people who love fishing, with a healthy mix of undercover police pretending to fish, but who are really just in Portaferry to hide from doing their job. There's never any crime in Portaferry. The main thing the Portaferrians think when looking across the water at Strangford Lough is, 'Why don't they just build a bridge across? If the ferry shuts down we're all fucked.'

A sidenote: Strangford Lough is not to be confused with Strang Ford, a local drunk of Portaferry, locked.

Another great reason to visit Portaferry is to take a look at the state of the art aquarium. It's the only aquarium in Northern Ireland. This isn't because the Northern Irish hate aquariums, far from it. The government decided to shut the rest of the aquariums down when fully grown men were eating popcorn and kept tapping at the glass, staring at the dolphins and calling them 'water-monkeys'. They thought it was a cinematic zoo. The only reason the aquarium remains in Portaferry is because it's illegal to eat popcorn in public here.

There's a holy well just outside Portaferry known as St Cooey's. This is a magical healing place that can cure all ailments, with one of the wells even having an inscription that says 'eyes' on it. Often suspected this water can cure blindness, upon further examination it turns out it actually just stings.

Namaste.

## Bangor

Bangor is a seaside town in the north of County Down. It's a haven for tourists who were too cheap to book a hotel in Belfast. This bustling port was first popularised by the Scottish and English planters who made their first stop in Bangor on their road to the plantation of Ulster. The national anthem in Bangor is 'Born Slippy' by Underworld. Usually followed by a lad in an Ellesse jacket saying 'aw mate, absolute Bangor'.

### What you'll find here

The Flagship shopping centre is an abandoned amusement park for consumers who love shops that are closed down. For years the Bangor natives have been baffled as to why shops in the Flagship keep closing down. It turns out once the Flagship closes at 7 p.m. it becomes an open-air waterpark full of bloodthirsty sharks that hate capitalism. And 13-year-old teenagers who break in and cause trouble because they want to rebel against their parents. Many of these teenagers sadly got swallowed whole by the sharks. Which has raised the average age of Bangor natives to 61.7 years old.

Pickie Park has been a family favourite of Bangorians ever since it opened its doors. It's a well-known destination for parents who are about to have a divorce in a last-ditch attempt to salvage their failing marriage. Everyone loves the swan boats in the park. They were a four-person paddling vehicle. Which was great news for a family of four, and bad news for a family of two parents and a child with an imaginary friend. If you go into Pickie Park on the seventh day of the seventh month on the seventh hour, you'll see the park empty, bar the swans paddling humans as an underappreciated form of poetic justice.

Another urban myth of Bangor is the council. It doesn't exist. This imaginary council have promised to revamp Bangor since the '90s. Their actions never materialise because nobody knows what the word 'revamp' means but they suspect it takes a lot of effort.

Namaste.

# COUNTY DUBLIN

People from Dublin think they're the centre of the universe. It's home to yupbros, D4s and Garda rats. There are literally no other type of people in Dublin. Dublin is a metropolis: a mixture of lads from DIT who can only understand each other by drunkenly shouting at 3 a.m. on Camden Street, lads who wore a facemask long before the pandemic, and southside girls who don't listen to you unless you use the word 'après ski' every 3.8 seconds on average. And hotels. Hotels everywhere.

# Top five things you don't want to miss:

## 1. Letting a stranger borrow your phone on Dublin Bus
This is an experience not to be missed. The cosmic gamble, did they really run out of credit? Will you ever get your phone back? Who are they ringing?

## 2. Petting a Canada goose
This is a unique Dublin experience. The Canada geese are usually a friendly bunch. Crowding around each other in flocks and speaking in their native tongue. It can be dangerous to pet a Canada goose out in the wild so make sure you develop trust with them first by giving them a peace offering: Amber Leaf.

## 3. Getting your chicken fillet roll swiped by a seagull on Henry Street
Take a walk along Henry Street in the city centre with one of the finest chicken fillet rolls that Dunnes Stores has to offer. Revel at the intelligence and majesty of the seagulls, who seem to know the exact moment you are about to take the first bite of your roll and swoop in before you get the chance to enjoy it.

## 4. Taking a ride on the LUAS red line
Why not take a ride on the Luas red line for an exhilarating experience like no other? The red line is an action-packed real-life interactive movie. Anything could happen. A horse might jump on board, or maybe a pregnant girl will light up a smoke and start screaming at people. OR maybe nothing will happen at all. That's all part of the excitement. Don't be distracted by the numerous ticket machines and the influx of ticket inspectors. Always remember, the LUAS is free!

## 5. Burritos
Burritos are completely taking over Dublin. They are seen as a status symbol amongst college students. For the true neoliberal Dublin experience, make sure to eat a burrito while hanging out of one of Dublin's many cranes.

**TOXICITY RATING: 8.9**

# Cabra

Cabra in Spanish means goat, and goat in Cabranese stands for 'Gerrup Ou A Dzah.' Cabra is divided into Cabra East and Cabra West. These two areas were in constant battle for superiority for centuries. The government created ecstasy pills in the '90s to unify the Cabronians and the newly formed alliance between East and West became known as the Bleedin' State of Cabra.

## What you'll find here

The land known as the Seventeen Shops is one of the most iconic historical sites in Cabra. People believe there are more than seventeen shops here but nobody has ever successfully counted them because they get distracted by the Domino's they keep forgetting is actually in Cabra. And seventeen is just far too much.

Clarkes bakery is Cabra's pride and joy. The breakfast rolls sold here have a certain magical quality to them. The bread is baked on site. Some say it's softer than a skater from Ashington. Scientists speculate that the coleslaw served in Clarkes comes from a different dimension, Finglas West, yup.

Cabra and Ashington are separated by a Garda station, this is so the Garda can turn Ashingtonians away at the border, to stop indie rocker kids from entering their death. Despite this definite dividing line, whenever there's a shooting or a robbery in Ashington, the newspapers magically turn Ashington into Cabra, through a process that's become known as Abrakecabra. The same border exists between Cabra and Stoneybatter. To stop the hipsters from entering, Cabra needed the backing of an entire army barracks.

## Urban myths and legends

It's well documented that Sudocrem was created by a Cabra man, originally called 'soothing cream' but then it got changed to Sudocrem because soothing cream was too difficult for the Cabronians to say, it was believed Sudocrem put Cabra on the map as a forerunner of Irish science but really it was just popular because everyone in Cabra used to wear a nappy. Sudocrem led to the development of the term pseudo, meaning someone who is fake trying to come across as real, such as a pseudointellectual or in other words, a college student in the smoking area of the Back Page in Phibsboro.

All the houses in Drumcliffe are at weird angles to the road to discourage joyriders from zipping up and down the estate, because if they crash into the wrong house they could get chopped in half by a two up two down. Once the weather reaches over twelve degrees in Cabra it alters the consciousness of the young adult males, who take their tops off and tie their Canada Goose jackets to their waist.

The Bogie Park is home to the bogies of Cabra. There used to be a skatepark here but it got shut down due to the Cabronians striking fear into the hearts of the emos. The real name of this park is John Paul the second, and the Cabronians believe they can't be arrested in this area just because the pope landed here in a helicopter a few decades ago. The vast open space in this park is the perfect place to walk a dog, but no one in Cabra walks their dog, they just take pictures of them.

Ashtown is a strange universe that exists on the border of Cabra, home to college students who emotionally blackmail their parents into paying the rent, and empty office blocks that overlook Finglas. Due to the upper-class nature of this built-up area it's often referred to as Cabrafornia.

Ashtown is usually a place people only go to for an apartment viewing and then never return because the rent is too expensive. Ashtown natives have a Supervalu and a gym so they never need to enter Cabra. There's a button in some of the more exclusive apartment complexes that allows the Ashtown residents to fast forward through the realm of Cabra on their journey into the city centre.

The KKC kickboxing club is a cult where Cabronians go to learn how to fight so they can go cause trouble in Finglas, or defend themselves to the death when someone spots that their Gucci runners are fake.

Wedged somewhere between the banks of the Royal Canal and the winding paths of the Phoenix Park, there's a light that never goes out. It's called McDonald's. McDonald's in Cabra. They say if you go in there on a quiet day and listen to the burgers sizzle on the grill, you can almost hear them say 'for fuck sake this place is a kip.' There is often a power struggle between the McDonald's bouncers and the forgotten children of Dunard, which usually results in one of the flock saying 'I'll get me older brother in here and he'll bleedin burst ye.'

## NIGHTLIFE

The Oasis is the main attraction of Cabra. A perfect place to go for tourists who are looking to experience the Irish lifestyle. The black décor on the exterior makes you focus on the personality that's held within its four walls. Oasis actually named themselves after the Oasis, Liam and Noel pretended to be from up the road, but when the bartender saw that neither of them could drink, everyone just assumed they were from Phibsboro and kicked them out. If that's not enough of a reason to visit, the Oasis is an eco-friendly bar, powered exclusively by body heat and swings of the jaw.

Namaste.

# Malahide

Young Malahidians have no concept of life outside Malahide. Most will stay in Malahide forever and refuse to grow into self-actualised human beings, because they think they're hard even though their parents are rich. These people are dangerous, like half dead wasps. They fear that if they don't sting you first, someone from Swords might kill them with a tennis racket.

All the young adults in Malahide walk around like their dad owns Tamangos. Their self-assured nature in the face of a lack of wisdom and life experience is often known as *Malapride* – a feeling of unearned self-belief that stems from living in Malahide. The elder Malahide natives suffer from a malady called Southside Syndrome. Their slogan is never let geography, or reality, get in the way of the truth. They believe Dublin 4 is just a number, a number that falls somewhere between Dublin 3 and early retirement.

## Urban myths and legends

The marina in Malahide was a government creation built so divorced men in their 50s could find a safe place to unbutton their shirt to an unacceptable level, revealing their unkempt chest hair while gazing out at the pier and pretending that just because they have money, that they don't actually have a drinking problem. The statue of the mermaid in the Marina is a symbolic gesture. Because it's much easier to give them a mermaid than it is to teach an entire village how to be a mermaid. Inside the statue of the mermaid is a hidden camera controlled by local resident Brendan Gleeson, who sits home and waits until the marina is quiet so he can walk his dog in peace.

## What you'll find here

Malahide Castle is the pride and joy of Malahide, for three days every summer when there's a festival on. But for the other 362 days of the year, Malahide Castle is just a backdrop for the main attraction of Malahide: Lady Acre, a sprawling field on the castle grounds that gets overrun by Malahidians who are trying to learn how to drink without getting sick. Lady Acre is a great place to get drunk and the forest is a great place to go missing.

Years ago the government installed train tracks in Malahide to split the area in half: separating the side that thinks they're from the ghetto from the posh side that isn't Seabury. Seabury have been trying to claim independence from the rest of Malahide since time began. And Malahide aren't against the idea either, trying to change their postal address to Swords, but Swords didn't want them. Because Seabury has too much Malahide in it to be accepted by somewhere that's not posh.

Millionaire's Row is one of Malahide's most sought-after residential areas. It's home to Boyzone's Ronan Keating, and Westlife's Nicky Byrne, who often go on jogs together just to be spotted. So that then people can post on the Malahide Facebook group saying 'I saw Ronan Keating and Nicky Byrne go on a jog together today' and no one will believe them. It's believed that you have to be a member of either a boy band or the illuminati to live on Millionaire's Row. Which is pretty much the same thing.

On a sunny day in the summer Malahide is overtaken by teenage Spanish students who don't really want to be in Malahide, they just like taking the bus out there to shout over each other and ruin the journey for everyone else.

Paddy's Hill is the highest peak in Malahide, even though it's really in Portmarnock – when it comes to Malahidians: the truth is irrelevant. Upon reaching the summit you'll find Paddy, and when you push him out of the way you can see the distant realms of Howth, the village Malahide is trying to be. The only way Malahidians can fulfil their lifelong dream of becoming accepted by Howth is by playing blackjack in the Westbury Casino, because the winner takes it all, and by all, I mean the winner gets to move to Howth. The local TDs in Malahide have promised that by 2025, enough Malahidians will have won big in the casino, to convince Howth to colonise the area completely.

## NIGHTLIFE

If you put your ear to the ground in Karpackie green, you can hear the rustling crinkle of an empty bag of coke blowing in the wind, and if you listen even closer you can hear the sound of a wheelie bin burning. The Seaburian ritual that happens every weekend which is the upmarket equivalent to incinerating a stolen car.

Gibney's is the main meeting point of Malahidians. This pub has been around since the late 1700s and they've always had the same staff, they just look younger because every time they overhear a drunken member of the yacht club wax philosophical about how nobody appreciates a tasteless display of wealth anymore, they age backwards.

Namaste.

## Kimmage

Kimmage is one of the greatest mysteries of the universe. For many years people have been curious about this little suburb. The only times I've ever seen it was on that Irish edition of Monopoly and on the front of the 83 Dublin Bus. For anyone reading this from further afield, don't worry, none of us know what Kimmage really is either. I've never met anyone from Kimmage and nobody I know knows anyone from Kimmage. My theory is that Kimmage does exist but it's surrounded by a magnetic field and every time someone from Kimmage tries to leave to tell the world that Kimmage is a real place they get sucked back into the vortex. Kimmage is just a state of mind, like anxiety, or hunger, or feeling close to your family. They say that every time you touch your nose someone from Kimmage is pretending to be from Terenure. If you're reading this from Kimmage – please, don't be a liar, no one is reading this from Kimmage. People from Kimmage are only allowed to consume Kimmage-related media, so they just stare at a blank screen for sixteen hours a day.

Namaste.

# Dún Laoghaire

Philosophers have often summarised Dún Laoghaire as Biarritz at the front, Bombay at the back. Dún Laoghaire is the only place name in Ireland that doesn't have an English translation. And as a result, nobody in Dún Laoghaire actually knows how to speak English. Dún Laoghaire has more abandoned shops in it than it does Dryrobe-wearing, fashionable sea-swimming Blackrock College graduates aggressively flaunting their gratitude on Instagram at 5.30 in the morning.

## Urban myths and legends

The entire economy of Dún Laoghaire was kept alive by John's corner shop. This shamanic temple graced spiritual nourishment upon all the native Dún Laoghaireans. It shut down in the summer of 2021 and opened up under new patronage, leaving the Dún Laoghaireans hopelessly strolling through the Southside realm, bereft of true purpose. The leader of this temple, John, has ascended beyond the human realm and no longer needs sleep. This shop used to be open 24/7, no one ever saw John leave or enter the shop. He simply stood behind the till and waited. John loved the art of the sale so much that he would even sell you things that didn't exist yet.

The East pier is one of Dún Laoghaire's most popular attractions. Dún Laoghaireans say if you didn't kick the lighthouse at the end of the pier, you never walked along the East pier. Unfortunately this means if you have no legs, the East pier is not the place for you, unless you have excellent upper body strength and you can crawl across it like a turtle. It's believed that the lighthouse at the end of the East pier is actually an intelligent life form and, although you'd never hear it over the crashing of the waves, every time it gets kicked it makes a noise like 'rrreeeaa.'

Nobody ever dares travel the barren wasteland of the West pier. The city council cleared this desolate landmass of all human activity so Ryan Tubridy could walk along it in peace. But this political manoeuvre has defeated its purpose, because now if someone ever wants to bump into Ryan Tubridy all they have to do is go to the west pier, and he will be the only one there.

The church wall is an infamous landmark in Dún Laoighaire: it's a mystical time portal where the marginalised Dún Laoghareieans go to get hammered: this is the only place in south Dublin where you'll find the successful matrimony between alcoholism and religion. The church wall is where you'll find god in the end of the next can of Linden Village.

The government installed a methadone clinic in Dún Laoghaire to dispatch service users from the inner city into Dún Laoghaire to remind the affluent Dún Laoghaireans of how lucky they are compared to people that are dying in front of them.

The Forty Foot is a secluded sanctuary on Dún Laoghaire harbour. The Forty Foot is actually 37ft tall but they rounded it up to forty because this was the average age of the struggling fathers trying to bond with their sons while having an identity crisis at the same time. The Forty Foot is full of people you would never want to know in real life. If that makes you question whether or not you know anyone that swims in the Forty Foot, don't worry, they never shut the fuck up about it.

Dún Laoghaire is powered by the most influential cult in the world: Scrumdiddly's. Scrumdiddly's put a secret ingredient in their ice cream that makes people queue up outside their shop for two hours for a 99 with a gummy bear in it. This social process is called scrumdiddification. Or, getting scrumdiddlied.

Dún Laoghaire is home to a lot of local Irish talent: much to his dismay, Ronnie Drew was actually from Dún Laoghaire, which, if we are to consider Dún Laoghaire and Dublin as two separate entities, which they aren't, means Ronnie Drew is from Dún Laoghaire, which means Ronnie Drew was from Dublin all along. Bob Geldof is also from Dún Laoghaire, but nobody really cares.

The skater kids of Dún Laoghaire love to wear ripped jeans, because buying pre-ripped jeans helps them to block the shame they feel about being born into a rich family. However, when the natives of Tallaght come down to the pier during the summer, the Dún Laoghaire skaters shrivel up and retract into the protective shell of Canterbury hoodies.

The Dún Laoghaire shopping centre is all business on the ground, first and second floor, and then on the third floor it's a vast expanse of empty space, due to the formation of a black hole that appeared inside the shopping centre in the late '90s. This sucked all the businesses on the third floor into its gaping vortex, all bar Peter Mark, who somehow escaped the spaghettification of Dún Laoghairean spacetime. Some believe this is because they sell an ancient relic known as 'hair straighteners'. Unfortunately, no one buys these ancient artefacts, because it's not 2009, you're not going to a Gaeltacht disco. A spaceship fell out of the starry Dún Laoghaire sky one night and while many have come to believe that it is a library, it's more commonly known as the Death Star of South Dublin. It's always empty and cost the taxpayer €48 million that could've been spent on housing, but at least Dún Laoghaire can say they have a spaceship.

Dún Laoghaire has reached its peak of civil unrest. And obviously, I am the only one who can restore equilibrium to this tangled web of postal codes. It's time to emancipate Dún Laoghaire and its surrounding clusters. Dún Laoghaire, no longer shall you exist solely to give the people of Sallynoggin, Glasthule, Monkstown and Sandycove imposter syndrome whenever they pretend to be from Dún Laoghaire on a night out in the city centre. Sallynoggin is actually not in Dún Laoghaire... if it was in Dún Laoghaire it would just be called Dún Laoghaire!

### NIGHTLIFE

O'Loughlin's is the oldest pub in Dún Laoghaire. Nobody ever goes in there except for the people that go in there, they all go in there. The lights are always off, the shutters are down and they don't have a cash register, O'Loughlin's is often referred to as the Schrödinger's cat of pubs. Namaste.

## Clondalkin

Years ago, Clondalkin used to be a sovereign state, known as the Republic of Clondalkia, but then they changed their name because they didn't want the area to sound more interesting than it actually is. Upon entering the realm of Clondalkin, it almost feels like you're in Clontarf, but as you get deeper into Clondalkin you realise you're definitely in Clondalkin. The war still wages on between Clondalkin village and Neilstown, and by war, I mean people from Clondalkin village run across the street and log out of their Revolut when they see a native of Neilstown approaching. Clondalkin used to be unified as one, but then Xtra-vision closed and the Clondalkians realised that life is a perpetual state of constant death.

### Urban myths and legends

Neilstown, also known as the real Clondalkin, has a Supervalu with a special chute for chicken fillet rolls that go directly from the deli to the cashier. Many got the impression that this was to discourage shoplifting, but it was actually just because the Supervalu in Neilstown was invented by a ten-year-old who was really good at Lego.

The round tower is the spiritual healing centre of Clondalkin. There were rumours that the Eurovision was meant to be held here but due to Clondalkin not actually being in Ireland and the fact that everyone in Clondalkin played football and didn't care about the Eurovision ... the rumours weren't actually true. The round tower was erected in the seventh century and is one of the four stone dildos in Dublin, with the others in Swords, Rathmichael and Lusk.

Ha ha ... Lusk!

The Round Tower GAA club is Clondalkin's international space station. They have a smaller round tower at the entrance to pay homage to the main round tower, 200 metres down the road. This mock round tower is actually a spacecraft that is controlled by voice command, it takes off once a year every Halloween when someone shouts 'gerrup ye lil' rocket'.

The people of Clondalkin have held firm against the oncoming riptides of cultural shifts that have ebbed and flowed through the rest of Dublin. The government tried to gentrify Clondalkin over the years and Clondalkin just laughed in their face.

The Happy Pear tried to muscle in on the Clondalkin landscape in 2017 but they closed permanently in 2020. If there's two things Clondalkians won't stand for, it's pears and happiness.

Not many people know that Clondalkin nearly became a Gaeltacht town in 2012 but their love of the Irish language became overshadowed by their fear of becoming fluent in Irish, while many Clondalkians know a cúpla focal, most of them know fuck all.

The Mill shopping centre is where Clondalkians go to spend their disposable income. And in the parking lot is where they go to have a mill. There is a European quality to this shopping centre, because no one really knows if it's inside or outside, but it doesn't matter because there's a huge Dunnes Stores at the back of the building, this Dunnes Stores is also known as Clondalkin South, and it has more security guards than it does people. The Mill shopping centre, in all its majestic modesty, still somehow has a better reputation than the shopping centre in Crumlin.

Right down the road you'll find what appears to be a local gym called Anytime Fitness, but it's not really a gym, it's a time portal you can enter that transcends reality and brings you back to a time when you were fit, and quite possibly, happy. Anytime Fitness teleports you back to your 16-year-old self, a time when you could walk up a flight of stairs without having to gasp for your life.

Clondalkin is home to many celebrities, celebrities who pretend to be not from Clondalkin. Graham Norton was born in Clondalkin but his parents moved him to Cork at the age of five to increase his chances of survival. Now he runs a talk show where he talks about everything except Clondalkin.

Experts agree there are only two places in Clondalkin: Cherrywood and Cherrywouldn't. Cherrywood is an estate in Neilstown, and

Cherrywouldn't is everywhere on earth that isn't Cherrywood, and as they say in Clondalkin, it's bleedin' massive.

## NIGHTLIFE

Clondalkin natives love to unwind. Legend has it that one New Year's Eve, they unwound so hard in Quinlan's bar that the ceiling had to be replaced. The Finches pub is the main attraction for Clondalkin-based tourism. Rumour has it the bouncer is dyslexic and thought it was called flinchin' and when he'd see a couple arrive he would say '2 for flinchin is it?' And then give them both a dead arm. Due to the lack of natural sunlight in this pub, Finches is known as the twilight zone of Clondalkin. Many souls have become lost to this metaphysical realm. Nobody in The Finches believes in the concept of time, the Finchians are the highest order of spiritual monks in the republic of Clondalkia: they believe it's never too early and it's never too late. It simply, is.

The Blue Banana nightclub was the home of the '90s Dublin rave scene, creating a contagion of adults who are now in their early forties and who still refuse to grow up. These prehistoric ravers wear vintage tracksuits that haven't been washed since 1994 and a cap that says *Rave 2 da grave*. Even though the club has been shut for years now, it's believed many of its attendees are still in search of their jaw.

Namaste.

## Balbriggan

Nobody knows where Balbriggan is, especially the people that live there. It's part of this imaginary place called 'Fingal County', a made-up land that only exists on signs at the side of the motorway. Balbriggan in Irish means 'no buses go here, turn back'. Balbriggan is stuck in a purgatory of Irish geography, unwanted by Dublin, with too many Dubs in it to be considered a part of Meath. Balbriggan: the eternal question mark. The long finger on the outstretched hand of urban sprawl.

Balbriggan have their own brand of KFC called FLC. FLC stands for Fuckin' Lovely Chicken. The car park near this knock-off KFC is where Balbrigganites go to have a knock off each other when the local nightclub closes.

If someone from Balbriggan doesn't know your name, instead of calling you 'yer man' they call you 'our lad' because deep down, whether we like it or not, we all, for some reason, belong to Balbriggan. 'Our lad' is the favourite phrase of the Balbrigganites, because the Socialist Republic of Balbriggan doesn't believe in the concept of private property.

Balbriggan is right beside an even more random place called Balrothery. Balrothery is Balbriggan's little brother. No one has heard of Balrothery until now. Balrothery is a ghost town, everyone who lives there is invisible. They will never forget the pain they feel for living in Balbriggan's shadow.

The Balbriggan and Skerries rivalry is a rivalry as old as rivalry itself. There has always been a class war between the two neighboring areas, with Skerries obviously winning. Balbriggan got jealous that Skerries had a beach so Balbriggan created their own beach purely out of spite. The seagulls in Balbriggan are chemically engineered to be so loud that the Skerriers scurry away from the harbour, due to their overly sensitive ears and general inability to adapt to the harsh realities of life.

The mystery of Balbriggan goes even deeper. Due to the Balbriggian natives being in a perpetual state of confusion, they're 73 per cent more susceptible to adopting strange spiritual beliefs, with one religious society in particular reigning over all the rest. The Cabana café. Somehow this quaint little gluten-friendly coffee shop has thrived in the Balbriggan climate, converting the locals to the religion of veganism with their non-pastry pastries and their deliciously long-sounding coffees with no caffeine in them. They play whale music to heighten the ambience in this haven of iced lattes, which drowns out the sounds of the gentrification.

# Blackrock

Blackrock got its name because they wanted to disguise the fact that it's full of rich white people. Blackrockians have their own distinctive speech. It's unique from the rest of Dublin. It sounds like the Southside on steroids. There are only men in Blackrock, they're known as the Blackrock boys, all the women in Blackrock are a simulation from Booterstown. No buses have ever been spotted in Blackrock. No one from Blackrock would ever be desperate enough to go anywhere. Due to the one-way system on their roads, you don't get to pick your own journey, you have to let Blackrock pick for you. An apt metaphor for the paved road of career opportunities in the area. You get to be a doctor, a lawyer or you get to get out and live in Sallynoggin.

The war between cyclists, drivers and pedestrians is the bane of Blackrockian existence. There are bicycle lanes everywhere in Blackrock, and due to the Blackrockian pedestrians being too consumed with 'absolutely sending it mate', they're too unobservant to focus on other moving carbon-based lifeforms, causing them to walk on the cycle path. This creates a dent in the social atmosphere of Blackrock, fuelling the cyclists with a primitive rage and a disdain for people who don't have bikes, seeing them as obstacles in their path. When a Blackrock cyclist unleashes their inner turmoil on an unobservant pedestrian, someone from Monkstown pretends they didn't go to Blackrock College. These cyclists became known as cycle-path psychopaths.

## What you'll find here

Blackrock has an impenetrable wall. It's taken me 200 years to be allowed into Bear coffee shop. This is where Blackrockians go to ensure that they have their daily dose of caffeine so that their illusion of productivity doesn't crumble.

There's a Supermac's in the middle of Blackrock. This was put there as an ironic joke, because Blackrock is precisely the opposite of Supermac's in every possible way. When you enter the Supermac's it's just a room full of empty space, but none of the Blackrockians ever found out because they've never been inside it. This particular Supermac's is a charging station for homesick UCD students from the countryside.

The Blackrock Market is where Blackrockians accentuate their social status. The market is known as Blackrock goes bohemian. The Blackrock Market is like any other market in an upper-class area, in that there is nothing that you'd ever really need here. The Blackrockians engage in competitive consumption patterns to try to outdo each other and see who can buy the most useless object. The winner gets to feel more important than everyone else. The slogan in the Blackrock Market is 'If you need it, it's not here.'

Blackrock calls everything Frascati to confuse outsiders and frighten them into running away. Up until now, no one knew why the shopping centre was called Frascati. People assumed that Frascati had a history, but Frascati is actually the name of a Blackrock College student who failed his Leaving Cert because he smoked too much weed. So his dad decided to name a shopping centre after him, to immortalise his legacy.

### NIGHTLIFE

Jack O Rourke's is the pub Blackrockians go to when they become too old to drink cans on the seafront. This is the pub where rock shandy was invented, and as a result, everyone from Blackrock truly believes this success had something to do with them. The pint of Heineken has become fetishised as a symbol of Blackrockian freedom. The Blackrock Boys are too sophisticated to simply go out for a few pints, instead they must light up a stick of Heinomite.

Namaste.

# Clontarf

Clontarf is arguably one of the poshest places on the northside, a real paradise in hell. An interesting fact about the natives of Clontarf is that no one ever talks to each other because they're too busy exercising and improving themselves. The early-morning joggers in Clontarf are actually simulations designed to make non-athletic Clontarfians feel bad about themselves for staying up all night drinking cans and doing coke. Clontarf is steeped in history. The 1014 Battle of Clontarf still wages on, but it's spread into Artane because no one from Clontarf knows how to fight.

## What you'll find here

Nolan's supermarket is the control centre of the Clontarf Moms. Nolan's is where you go if you want to pay double the amount you'd pay for anything anywhere else. The premium you pay is the cost of admission into the Clontarf Mom ecosphere. The Clontarf Moms are all extensions of the same person, a blonde-haired hot yoga mom with a white fluffy dog. Clontarf Moms are only allowed talk about four topics: their children, their husband, their holidays and themselves. If you try to have a deep meaningful conversation with a Clontarf Mom their eyes turn black and you can see the words 'GET OUT' written in their pupils. It's believed that if you scratch the surface of a Clontarf Mom, you'll find a wounded woman who was outpriced from Howth.

The fabled kiosk of Happy Out found its way into Clontarf only a few years ago. They even built a wooden bridge so that people would have to exercise to get a flat white.

Mattress Mick is the spiritual leader of Clontarf. There's a genetic code inside Clontarfian natives that makes them so obsessed with Mick that whenever they spot him, they have to either announce it to the public or take a picture with him. Due to Mattress Mick being collared by Clontarfian technology, studies suggest Mattress Mick is a shapeshifting entity and has often been in two or three places at the exact same time.

St Anne's Park is the unruly ecosystem of Dublin 3. Or is that Fairview? St Anne's is the ancient divide between Clontarf and Raheny. Everyone from Clontarf starts their underage drinking career on Pitch 21. For the first few years, these Clontarfians all fight amongst each other for dominance, although around the age of sixteen, their prospective hopes are shattered by Coolockians and Harmonstinians, who commandeer the vicinity to beat them up and steal their cans. It's usually around this time that these Clontarfians suddenly realise there's no point fighting, it's at this point, the Clontarfians suddenly realise they're from Clontarf. These young Clontarf natives migrate to drinking indoors in their friends' houses, where their can-stealing enemies will be unable to make it past the password-protected electric gate.

Namaste.

## Phibsborough

Geographically speaking, no one knows where Phibsborough begins. It's simply known as the almond-milk-latte version of Cabra: the Rathmines of the Northside. Phibsborough in Irish roughly translates to 'the eternal coffee shop'. People from Phibsbourough think they need to spell Phibsborough in two different ways. Because if they just called Phibsborough 'Phibsborough', then Phibsboro would feel left out. In *Time Out* magazine, Phibsborough ranked as one of the coolest neighborhoods in the world to live in because it has the perfect combination of struggling college students, Deliveroo drivers and the criminally insane.

### Urban myths and legends

The Eddie Rocket's in Phibsborough is the best Eddie Rocket's in Ireland to charge your phone in, but only if you're in Phibsborough and there's no other Eddie Rocket's to choose from. The McDonald's across the road barely has any food in it, this is because they're just pretending to be a McDonald's. It's really a top-secret international space station powered by the pizza place next door. So secret, that I'm the only one who knows about it.

The annual Phizzfest has been baffling Phibsboreans for centuries. We've all seen the posters go up, but why has no one ever been there? What happens there? Is it a cult?

The redbricks and mortar of Dalymount Park has weathered the storm of gentrification. This is where the old Phibsorough residents go to recapture the spirit of what Phibsborough used to be, before it turned into a giant piece of avocado toast.

James Kavanagh is the King of Phibsborough. During the day he lives inside the big Tesco and at night time he sleeps in his car, draped in a

Dryrobe, surrounded by melting Yankee candles and his cat. Phibsborough is basically a glorified Instagram ad.

No one knows what's inside Phibsborough shopping centre. This 1960s shopping complex is a glitch in the video game of Dublin 7. Every time you go deeper into the heart of this Phibsborean jungle your journey restarts from your last checkpoint, Tesco. The local TDs promise every year the centre will get a makeover, but instead they accidentally agreed to turn it into a co-living space. The government decided to swallow up all the charity shops in the area and replace them with coffee shops, to see if flat whites could cure homelessness. It turns out they can't, but now Phibsborough boasts the most caffeinated homeless people in the country.

Phibsborough is split into two camps: Old Phibsborough and New Phibsborough. Old Phibsborough are the residents who've lived there for generations and New Phibsborough are the people who've migrated to the area due to a recommendation on a Top 10 list on JOE.IE. The end goal of New Phibsborough is to cordon off Old Phibsborough, bullying them into a small circle. A small circle called Cabra.

Back in 2018, whenever someone said 'lets go to the Canal', they meant the Grand Canal in Portobello, but ever since the Bernard Shaw relocated to Phibsborough, going to the canal became known as the Royal Canal in Phibsborough, because the Bernard Shaw is the dictator of the way the water flows. The Royal Canal became so normalised that it lost its prefix and now it's just the Canal. Before the Bernard Shaw moved to Phibsborough, the Phibsboroeans claimed they drank cans at the Canal all their life, but they were just living out a demented fever dream, to protect them from realising they were actually drinking Dutch Gold in their room, because the Canal hadn't been invented yet.

## *NIGHTLIFE*

McGowans is the charging station of Phibsborough residents. This is where they drunkenly mingle with Glasnevians and Drumcondraeans. The bouncers here make sure the Broadstonians and Cabrasites get stopped at the door because the regulars are too afraid of them.

The Back Page is the home of the Hipsters of Phibsborough. Everyone wonders what book the Back Page was taken from. Some believed it was ripped from the NCAD student manual. The Back Page has schizophrenia. It doesn't know if it's a restaurant, a sports bar or a smoking area. All that's for sure is once you enter through these doors you won't leave without letting everyone know how confused you are. The Back Page has a magic spray doused around the entrance that blinds you if you're a Bohs fan.

Namaste.

## Swords

Some say Swords is the real capital of Dublin and others say Swords is Blanchardstown's posh little cousin. Apparently 40,000 people live in Swords. But who are these people? Why doesn't anyone know them in real life? By law of averages, about 4 per cent of Dublin are from Swords. But here we are, trying to find out how all these people from Swords have passed us by, virtually undetected. If you ever want to find out once and for all if you're in the presence of a Swordsinian there are a few tell-tale signs. The young males of Swords are all aspiring Soundcloud rappers who pretend to like UK drill music and start shouting 'Yup Swords' anytime they go outside the Swords border; this is their battle cry, their call to arms that rouses other Swords natives in the area out of their slumber. The females of Swords all have similar hand tattoos alongside their similar Instagram pages of similar makeup tutorials.

### Urban myths and legends

The Pavilions shopping centre is genetically imprinted into the minds of Swords natives at birth; their primary caregiver is the shopping centre, which is why people from Swords don't feel close to their families. They pin their hopes and dreams on this decaying relic of consumerism. From a young age, they hang around outside the McDonald's until the high-pitched ringing noise starts and the security guard moves them along. The Pavilions is where the Swordsinians go to laugh, to celebrate and to cry when they are feeling undermined by worldly problems, like not fitting into the ecosystem of Malahide.

Swords is the takeaway capital of the world. There's a takeaway to human ratio of 2:1, so for every person in Swords there are 2 takeaways. Meaning if you don't want the driver of your local takeaway to know how much you struggle to cook for yourself, you can just order from the other takeaway, so both drivers only think your life is half the mess that it really is.

Swords is steeped in history, but perhaps the most ancient battle of them all is the battle for the Jacko. The Jacko is now a park but it used to be a sanctuary full of mystical creatures such as the chieftain of Swords: Bill Cullen. Bill gathered his riches by dousing himself in war paint and charging people 3 euro a pop to enter the Jacko while beating on a drum with a sock full of wet cement just before jumping into a helicopter to give a motivational talk to a primary school down the country. The war between Swords Manor and River Valley has reverberated through the Jacko for centuries. Both sides seem to claim the Jacko belongs to them. The Jacko has been the great divider of Swords, the enchanted land where battles are lost and bottles are broken. Some day the people of Swords Manor and River Valley will stop fighting over the Jacko and join forces to create a new Swordsian dynasty called Swalahide. It'll be a hybridisation of Malahide and Swords. And Malahide will move to the Southside, where it truly belongs.

Swords is home to two Lidls and two Aldis, which makes Swords the middle aisle of County Dublin. Yet perhaps the most iconic element in the alloy of Swords culture was the JC supermarket. The JC was once a bastion of hope from the roaring Celtic Tiger. The Swordsian sense of self is inextricably linked with this supermarket. The JC has since become a shadow of its former self when it was taken over by Dunnes Stores. The JC stands for Jesus Christ. But Jesus Christ when Dunnes Stores came along, no one stood up for Jesus.

Despite the humble offerings of the mostly empty 41 bus, the true method of public transportation is the Swords Express. The Swords Express is a magical road-bound teleportation device that transits Swords natives to places that are not in Swords. The reason it's called Swords Express is because it's free to get on but the price you pay is you have to get up the front of the bus and express yourself. Tell everyone your secrets and then sit there in the hour it takes to get into town listening to your headphones while wondering if everyone thinks you're a freak.

## NIGHTLIFE

People often wonder what happened to the Wright Venue. Some think the people of Swords rallied together and got rid of the nightclub because they were tired of drunk teenagers getting sick in their garden after last orders. But the truth is Wright's was actually a lab where the Swords natives were created and dispatched to the rest of Dublin from. People started realising that you could never imagine what a Swords lad who loves going to Wright's would do on a Tuesday night and it was too much to think about so Wright's got shut down as a preventative measure. No one could really imagine what an overly-friendly, kind of annoying lad pretending to be on drugs would be like when he's not in Wright's, being overly friendly, kind of annoying and pretending to be on drugs in Wright's.

Namaste.

# Ballyfermot

Ballyfermot is more commonly known as Ballyer. Which comes from the Latin word Ballyfermus, which directly translates to 'man with leash walking goat'.

Ballyfermot is the place where the commuter belt unbuckles to take a piss all over its own leg. And it feels great. Since the dawn of time Ballymun, Ballybrack and Ballybough have tried to claim the title of Ballyer but Ballyfermot has always been the true Ballyer. And Ballyfermot is the only real Ballyfermot in Ballyfermot. Ballyer existed, long before Ballyfermot ever began. The term Ballyfermot was just a social construct created to make Ballyer sound posh when they were on the phone to Chapelizod. Ballyfermot is a hub of creativity: home of the Fureys, Mary Byrne, Andy Reid and Glenn Whelan, who didn't actually get his second name from his parents, he got it because he loves rippin' wheelies with the lads on the weekend; his parents are actually Mary Byrne and Andy Reid.

## Urban myths and legends

It's believed that there is a secret code inside the battered Oreos in the local chipper, B Borza. Once the battered Oreos are consumed by a non-Ballyfermot native, the Ballyfermians can suddenly hear your thoughts. They know you're asking yourself why the fuck are there so many horses around here.

## What you'll find here

Ger's Deli is the beating heart of Ballyfermot. Scientists often wonder what came first, the Deli or the Ger. It's now believed that they both happened at the same time. Ger used to run this deli with his friend Dan, and they decided to put their names together and call it DanGer's Delicatessen, but when Dan started eating all the hashbrowns out of the stockroom Ger kicked him out and painted over the letters at the front of the shop and then it became Ger's Deli.

Iceland is a true staple of Ballyfermian life. Ancient historians suggest this store is the oldest Iceland in the world. Older than Iceland itself. Iceland saw what Iceland was doing and they decided to make a country out of it. The original descendants of Iceland are all from Ballyfermot. And they're fucking freezing.

At the heart of Ballyfermot lies Cherry Orchard. This is the best place to go if you are an American tourist looking for a day of picking cherries in the beautiful local forest with the occasional rustic aesthetic of a burnt-out Honda Civic.

The gods of Ballyfermot decided to put an art college in the middle of Ballyer as a social experiment to see how the locals would react to having sulky teenagers in their mid-20s from Stillorgan make abstract animation about global warming and BDSM. Ballyfermot also has a rock school, which was erected in 1998. It was formed from the power of the sweat of Christy Moore's left armpit. The college was originally called Christy Moore's music school, which was named after Christy Moore, who was named after Christy Moore's music school. But when Christy Moore found out that most of the students of the music school were too indie to know who he is, Christy would wait outside the walls of the college every day for the entire winter pretending to read the Communist Manifesto and would offer the students a smoke as they passed by, just before guilting them into listening to his folk mixtape.

### NIGHTLIFE

Chasers is the local pub of Ballyfermot, the epitome of the Ballyfermian imagination. Chasers has a screening test at the door where a robot runs a swab to monitor the salt of your neck sweat and if your levels aren't high enough they don't allow you to enter. Due to Ballyfermians being naturally hard workers their neck sweat has excess levels of salt in it, so this simple test stops outsiders from the local college from intruding upon the Ballyfermian space. Every so often the machine malfunctions and a handful slip through the cracks and enter the pub. They soon get chased out by a legion of angry Ballyfermians brandishing pool cues and roaring mouths full of chewed-up peanuts. This is how the pub became known as Chasers.

Namaste.

# Lucan

Lucan is one of the biggest suburbs in Dublin. About one in every three people on earth are either from Lucan or have lived in Lucan. That includes people who have never lived in Dublin at all. Thirty per cent of Lucanites are currently lost, looking for their house, because all the estates here look the exact same. And due to there only being about four pubs in the area, everyone feels like they are lost together. If you tell someone you're from Lucan they will always give you the same response: 'Nacul', which is Lucan spelled back to front. Nacul is the natural reaction people give you when they pretend not to judge you for being from a place that isn't sure if it's in Leixlip or in despair. The young males of Lucan are an interesting bunch. Not interesting, but predictable at least. Young men from Lucan have only three life aspirations: to be a gym instructor, a barber or a DJ. It is possible for these young adult males to be interested in more than one of these hobbies at once, or even perhaps, fluctuate between the three, but no one from Lucan has ever been interested in anything else. The end goal of these Lucan males is to become a contestant on *Love Island*.

## What you'll find here

Amidst the barren wasteland of similarity lies Liffey Valley. Liffey Valley is the centre of Lucan, the centre of Lucan that just so happens to be in Clondalkin. It's a shopping temple controlled by Lucan's ancient warlords John and Edward, who rule over the people of Lucan with an iron fist.

The question of the estate of Balgaddy has been puzzling historians for years – it's the no man's land between Clondalkin and Lucan. Claimed by neither, rejected by both. One could argue that 'Balgaddy has no Daddy.'

Just south of Lucan lies the mysterious village of Adamstown. Adamstown is a government creation: it's the most realistic and least interesting video game ever created. The state wanted to see what would happen if they created a satellite town and filled it with non-playable characters.

You may remember spending time in Fort Lucan. No you didn't. Fort Lucan didn't exist, it was just a data centre of false memories created to make you think you had a successful childhood. You weren't on a water-slide, you were actually just screaming into the void in a shopping centre, crying for your mother, who you thought had abandoned you, which, as it so happens, is the only natural response to being trapped in Lucan.

Namaste.

# Tallaght

People from Tallaght think Tallaght is the most magical place on earth. But from an objective point of view, the only thing magic about Tallaght is how it transforms from a Southside suburb to Dublin West as soon as something goes missing.

## Urban myths and legends

The Square shopping centre is actually in the shape of a pyramid. The Square, was there since time began. Some believe it was built by Tallaght's very own Richard Dunne just so he could get up on the roof and play heads and volleys by himself without people interrupting him to ask him why is he on top of the Square shopping centre playing heads and volleys by himself.

The entire economy of Tallaght is powered by the Domino's in the Square, The workers here are so fast on the floor that the steam from their body heat turns the place into an accidental sauna. Reports suggest that it's the busiest Domino's in the world, but it was really just a clever tactic to stop unruly Domino's enthusiasts from roaring down the phone at some poor fifth-year student about having to wait an extra five minutes for their Mega Deal.

Tallaght natives often used to report that they could smell biscuits when approaching the Jacob's factory, but when it closed in 2015 and was replaced by Amazon, the biscuit smell still remained. It turns out Tallaght actually just smells like biscuits.

The Jobstown River is perhaps one of the most underrated tourist attractions in Tallaght. It's more radioactive than watching your food cook in a microwave in Chernobyl. It's toxic to the human touch. But it's a really good place to wash your sneakers. Parents used to scare their children by warning them if they spent too much time swimming in the river, someday they'd end up on Tallafornia.

The age-old question of Firhouse has been argued for centuries. Is it really in Tallaght? The final answer is: Firhouse is actually in Firhouse, and Firhouse is in Tallaght. Firhouse is the safety net that stops people from Tallaght from entering Rathfarnham. The first line of defence that protects the rest of south Dublin from the yupbros of the south-west. Deep down, Firhouse is just Tallaght in denial.

## NIGHTLIFE

Perhaps the greatest culture war of all time was the battle between Tallaght's two nightclubs: Show and Entourage. Every Saturday night when the clubs closed, both groups would congregate in the McDonald's and the surrounding car park and engage in what can only be described as a riot of extinction-level carnage: the Hunger Games of Dublin 24. The bleedin'-starvin' get-outta-my-way games. The winner got to skip the queue and order the first Big Mac while also being awarded with the privilege of seeing the unbridled look of fear in the eyes of the outnumbered Gardaí, as they stood there and did nothing. Because they were frightened.

Namaste.

## Rathmines

Rathmines is a middle-class simulation of the inner city. It's often been called Camden Street's fake eyelashes. Just with less drunk culchies and more parched Yoga Moms perching over a park bench, drinking iced caramel lattes and pretending to keep an eye on their children. Rathmines is one of those places that I'd always gaze over at when I used to drink cans by the canal in Portobello. I'd look over and I'd wonder 'Why the fuck is there a building there that looks like the Taj Mahal?' and then I'd snap out of it and realise the building is probably looking back at me thinking 'Who's that lad in the weird tracksuit drinking Tesco Lager by himself?'

## Urban myths and legends

It's believed that people from Rathmines have their own language. They use phrases like 'flat deece' and 'fulla notions'. These words were invented by Lovin' Dublin and they don't actually mean anything but are often used to distinguish Rathminians from people from Harold's Cross. Lovin' Dublin socially engineered these phrases to make gentrification seem like an exciting new vegetable you'd find at Fallon & Byrne's. Lovin' Dublin originally intended for Rathmines to be a hashtag but then it started to occupy space in the physical realm when a handful of art-film directors began to inhabit the area, sitting outside coffee shops all day talking about themselves really loudly.

Rathmines has come on in leaps and bounds over the years. It used to be full of bedsits, and it still is, but the struggling families that once lived in the tenements have been replaced by disillusioned DIT students who thought they were supposed to be going to college on Aungier Street and instead shell out €850 a month to sleep on top of a wardrobe.

The Swan Centre is the most beautiful existential crisis of a shopping experience available to the modern-day consumer. Much like the swan itself, upon being in its presence you are taken aback by its elegance, but you're not sure if it's a good idea to get too attached to it, because some day it might decide to make like a swan and swim into a lake. This is obviously something that could happen, seeing as the Swan Centre is the only waterproof shopping centre in Ireland.  In the Swan Centre you can find everything you don't need. If it's unnecessary then you can be sure they have it here, and they probably have two or three shops where you can get it. But if you're looking for bread and milk, go to Templeogue or somewhere, no one here cares!

There used to be two Starbucks in Rathmines because the government thought that if there was twice as many Starbucks people would drink twice as much coffee. But it didn't work out and Starbucks ran Starbucks out of business. Now Starbucks is the only Starbucks left.

There are so many Mexican restaurants in Rathmines the ancient proverb states 'If you fling a fajita from the Little Ass Burrito Bar in Rathmines and no one is around to hear it, it still smashes the window of Tolteca.'

The Clocktower in Rathmines appeared one day out of nowhere and everyone just pretended it was always there because they didn't want anyone else to realise they were slowly going insane. The clock has four faces. One for every day of the week. It's believed that if you look directly into the north face of the clock tower at 5pm, it creates a dent in the symmetry of Rathminian reality, causing someone from Ranelagh to look directly at the clock and still ask you if you know what time it is, because people from Ranelagh don't know how to read clocks.

Rathmines also has a cinema. But it's a cinema full of lamps that serves cocktails in it, and then, in a form of social class guilt, they downplayed their privilege by calling the cinema 'Stella'. Rathmines happens to be home to the poshest McDonald's in Dublin. It's believed that after using the toilet an automated message plays over the intercom that says, 'thank you, we cherish your toxic waste.'

It's believed a lot of people from Rathgar are pretending to be from Rathmines so no one knows that they are actually from Rathgar, but if people knew they were from Rathgar, then no one would believe they were from Rathmines. Because they aren't. The general rule of thumb here is: just because it walks like a duck, and quacks like a duck, doesn't mean it went to St Mary's. These secret Rathgar natives often give themselves away, because a true Rathminian would never carry a copy of the *Irish Times* around with them everywhere they go and brag about how many skiing trips they've been on with their cousin Marius in the last five years. A real Rathmines native would be too busy effortlessly blending into the smoking area of the Bernard Shaw, pretending they don't have a rich family and talking about how many times they almost died in Berlin.

## NIGHTLIFE

The Blackbird is one of the cherished meeting places of Rathminian creatives: they congregate in this adult playground and talk about the podcast they're thinking of starting while they clutch onto the jam jar that cradles the content of some Canadian IPA they can't afford. Scientists believe they are trying to make it last as long as the dirty looks they get for still having a handlebar moustache at the age of thirty-two.

From Rathgar to Ranelagh. From Tramco to Lidl. Rathmines will continue to flourish as the multicultural Mecca amongst the sleepy suburbs of Dublin 6.

Namaste.

# Blanchardstown

Blanchardstown have been trying to gain independence from the rest of Dublin 15 ever since they magically grew a shopping centre out of the ground in 1996. The Blanchardstown people, or the Blanchardstinians, worship the Blanchardstown shopping centre, and see it as the omni-present force at the centre of their universe. If you took the shopping centre away from Blanchardstown all that'd be left are a couple of Lidls, the National Aquatic Centre and a bunch of housing estates full of people who want to go back to the Blanchardstown shopping centre.

## Urban myths and legends

The mystical power that keeps Blanchardstown alive is the 39a bus. This bus says Ongar on it but nobody stays on long enough to see if it actually goes there, so as far as anyone knows, Blanchardstown is the final stop. The 39a is the king of all 39-related buses. Distantly followed by the 39. Which goes so slowly that when you step on board time actually moves backwards and you end up further away from your destination than you were when you began your journey.

To anyone from Castleknock or Carpenterstown who need to hear this: the people of Blanchardstown would appreciate it if you could stop pretending to be from Blanch to sound hard. The Blanchardstinians would like to build a wall around their continent to protect themselves from shams like you.

### NIGHTLIFE

Even though the real heart of Blanchardstown is the Bell pub, the Bell pub is actually in Blanchardstown village. Which is not really Blanchardstown, because it's Blanchardstown village. And everyone knows Blanch village and Roselawn aren't really in Blanchardstown. This area is commonly known as Blanchardsknock: too posh for Blanchardstown and too Blanchardstown for Castleknock. It exists in this purgatory of social class and it doesn't want to do anything to change.

A few years ago it seems the Wetherspoons fell out of the sky and landed in Blanchardstown, tactically placed opposite the AIB. Today it's believed this is a false memory collectively shared by the Blanchardstown natives. Wetherspoons was actually always there. Even if the urban myth is that there used to be a nightclub here called Light that had an annual beach party that had so much bacteria floating about that the entire place had to be detonated.

Namaste.

# Ongar

Ongar is a new suburb that seemed to appear out of nowhere. Some people believe that Ongar is a social experiment – a simulation of what Blanchardstown would be like if it didn't have a shopping centre or any people living there. The houses in Ongar aren't actually real. Nobody lives in them. They are just the background of a movie set that never got made. Nobody really knows where Ongar is. Some say it's in Dublin, others say it's in Meath, but we can all agree that when you see the 39a bus with 'Ongar' written on it, your first thought is, 'I don't think I'll ever have a reason to go there'. But then I accidentally ended up living in Ongar for six months. And I had to get that bus everyday. And so did my friends whenever they wanted to come see me. It took an hour to get in from town and soon they stopped seeing me and began to hate me for it.

It wasn't because we drifted apart due to my unhinged, unpredictable nature.

It was definitely Ongar's fault.

Ongar is wedged between Clonsilla and Clonee. If you think of this trifecta of Dublin 15 as a sandwich, Clonee and Clonsilla are the two slices of bread, and Ongar is the unfamiliar meat substance in the middle. Not many people are eating that sandwich.

## What you'll find here

Ongar is home to all the taxi drivers in Dublin. In the last Census it was found there is an average of 1.4 taxi drivers per household in Ongar. They sign a secret contract when they become taxi drivers that uproots them from their area and moves them to Ongar. Nobody knows why the taxi companies make them do this but rumour has it that they just thought it'd be funny.

Ongar's saving grace is the Dunnes Stores in the middle of the village. This is where the locals go to do their pretend shopping to make you think they actually live here. It's almost convincing, but if you ask the staff where the eggs are, nobody will be able to tell you, because they don't really work there. This is all a show put on for your benefit.

Ongar just discovered what podcasts are. Someone with dyslexia was looking at a sign that said Ongar and he got the letters jumbled up and he thought it said Rogan and then he put it into Google and found some middle-aged bald guy talking into a microphone about the benefits of ayahuasca.

Ongar is a journey not a destination. You either pass through it to get to Blanchardstown or you live there until you can afford to move out. Ongar, keep being yourself. We appreciate your mysterious qualities, don't let us get to know you. Don't let us get too close. We like to keep on guessing.

Namaste.

# Knocklyon

Knocklyon is a quiet suburb in South Dublin. It's commonly known as the place you'll always end up at an aftersession with complete strangers only to leave at 8 in the morning without your phone charger. Then somewhere on the way to the bus stop you'll wonder 'Why the fuck am I in Knocklyon?'

You wage that internal battle of grave indecision, the ultimate conquest; do you swallow your pride and go back and get your phone charger or do you move on with your life? But of course you'd never go back once you've left and plus, those unruly Knocklyonians probably huddled around it and ate it.

## Urban myths and legends

Knocklyon is so quiet that they don't need a neighborhood watch service. Instead they have session view. This is a recreational activity where Knocklyonians peer out of a crack in the window in the small hours of the morning to watch confused outsiders traverse the Knocklyon ecosystem as they slowly come to terms that they're in the middle of nowhere and have no idea how to get home. While this activity offers some mild respite to these Knocklyonians in the moment, watching people trying to escape out of Knocklyon to leave an aftersession for years has gnawed away at the Knocklyonian collective consciousness. Which created an irreparable dent in the self-esteem of the Knocklyonian people.

The most interesting thing about Knocklyon is the more you say the word Knocklyon the less it makes sense until it becomes a meaningless glob of letters jumbled up together. Knocklyon, Knocklyon, Knocklyon, Knocklyon, kNOcklyon. Try it!

All there is in Knocklyon is a supermarket and a treatment centre, which is actually everything you need in a place that has nothing in it. The media try to sell Knocklyon as a desirable location, saying things like 'Priced out of Templeogue? Why not try Knocklyon?' which is like saying 'Fancy a night in a five-star hotel? Why not try a tent in Athlone?'

Knockylon also has a temple. It's locally known as the shrine of Knocklyon. It's an altar dedicated to famous people from Knocklyon, but because nobody famous is from Knocklyon, the famous people from Knocklyon were actually not from Knocklyon. The Knocklyonians had to use their imagination. Anyone can be from Knocklyon if you believe hard enough. Some of the celebrities featured in the shrine of Knocklyon include Blindboy, Gerry Adams and Damien Duff, who is actually Robbie Keane's brother.

## A note to the people of Knocklyon

Don't be upset because most of us try to escape you, you can see where we're coming from. Even you'll admit that Knocklyon is about as random as it gets. You're so far away from everything. I know you're right beside Tallaght but still. You seem like you're in a different county and there's just nothing we can do to change that. The bus from Knocklyon takes so long to get into town that by the time I reach O'Connell Street I've actually changed as a person. A different person that still has no intention of ever returning to Knocklyon.

Namaste.

## Stoneybatter

Stoneybatter used to be the centre of old Dublin. But over the last ten years it's become gentrified with student accommodation, expensive brunch spots and craft beer. Stoneybatter has been invaded by the hipsters. Due to Stoneybatter's allure of an alternative lifestyle this area has become a Mecca for creative people. But mostly, a Mecca for people who think they're creative just because they have creative friends and they aren't good at anything else. Broke college students are also literally dying to live here; the rent is so high that many students are living in unfurnished box rooms on Manor Street and literally starving to death.

## Urban myths and legends

Artisanal sourdough bread has become the national emblem of Stoneybatter. This brunch item was used as a weapon of social class division. Serving to draw in the middle-class hipster crowd while alienating the people who've lived there for generations, because it's always good to make people feel unwelcome in the home that you've pushed them out of.

The hipsters of Stoneybatter can be found congregating in the Belfry sipping on their expensive IPAs while they co-ordinate how they are going to gain independence as a sovereign state away from the rest of Dublin as well as the original non-hipster residents of Stoneybatter.

According to news reports and the extortionate rent prices, there is no crime in Stoneybatter. Not a single case has ever been reported. Every time a fixie gets stolen in Stoneybatter, they just say it happened in Cabra. If that's not enough to account for the high rent prices, the 30 per cent premium you pay in Stoneybatter is justified because of its symbol of status. It's worth it when all you have to say to people is 'I just moved into Stoneybatter' for them to think you're an NCAD graduate whose trust fund is running low while you pretend to be able to afford avocado toast for the rest of your life.

To the invading hipsters of Stoneybatter: you're not intimidating anyone with your eco-friendly CBD coffee, your vintage synthesizers or your forward-thinking, gluten-free sesame-seed bagels. You don't have to leave but please, no one needs to overhear you loudly profess your love for the Fairtrade granola in your wicker basket that you bought at the local farmers' market. Some people are trying to struggle in silence under the weight of an Ireland whose wings are burning as it flies too close to the European sun. So please just keep it down. Stop acting like Stoneybatter needs you. Acknowledge there was a culture that existed here long before the culture festival.

Just because you injected hipster customs into Stoneybatter, that doesn't give you the right to teach it back to the people who've lived there for generations.

You don't get to call Stoneybatter a multicultural society if you walk out of the shop with a kale smoothie in your hand and you don't give the homeless man outside the Centra any more than your pure contempt as you zip away on your electric scooter.

Namaste.

# Marino

Marino is a suburb on the Northside of Dublin. Marino has a rich history: it was the Irish state's first attempt at public housing back in the 1920s, but now it's basically just a glorified Tesco Express.

## Urban myths and legends

Casino Marino is a local landmark. Even though it's not really a casino and everyone just looks at it from a distance and says 'I must go in there someday' before completely forgetting about it. This weird-looking castle was built as a brothel for Lord Charlemont back in 1759. Upon entering this non-casino, you're asked to take your shoes off at the door. Some say this is so the rare Scandinavian wood on the floors of this non-casino doesn't get damaged, but it's actually just because the staff have a foot fetish. It's rumoured there are secret tunnels underneath the Casino Marino that were built so Michael Collins could test out guns underground away from the watchful eye of British soldiers, but when they were shooting their weapons, everyone heard them. The tunnels suddenly served a separate purpose. So that Michael Collins could practise running away from British soldiers. The people who live beside the casino have suffered for centuries. They're sick of everyone thinking Casino Marino is in Marino, when it's clearly in Donneycarney.

The Dublin Bus that goes through Marino is the 123 bus. Two thirds of its commuters are just curious people who say to themselves 'Wow, 123. I wonder where this bus will bring me.'

The C&T Superstore is one of the most loved places in Marino. It's a mini-market with great bargains and weird sunglasses. 95 per cent of the Marino locals have found employment in the C&T at some point in their lives. This shop is independently run by local hero Charlie, who has a throne at the centre of this store where the Marino locals bring him gifts. Usually gifts that they bought in the shop. It's a great spot for everyone who got barred from the Tesco in Fairview.

### NIGHTLIFE

There is a great war raging through the heart of Marino. It's the battle between BRÚ House and Gaffney's. BRÚ House is the foothold of Marino gentrification, serving craft beer and alternative comedy gigs. This is where you'll accidentally get stuck talking to someone from Raheny about how he used to listen to metal music before getting heavily into Tame Impala and DMT. The walk of shame from the men's toilet to the smoking area makes it feel like the bouncers are constantly looking at you, ready to kick you out at a moment's notice for accusing you of doing coke in the stall. Because you were, and they are. Gaffney's is the polar opposite of BRÚ House, full of creamy Guinness and county jerseys every day of the week. Some would argue that BRÚ House and Gaffney's aren't really in Marino, but they all agree that the best pubs in Marino are in Fairview.

If you're looking to go to a pub more classically Marino, try Marino House. This is a pub for the Marino purists, the perfect place for the Marino natives that are xenophobic towards the surrounding areas of Dublin 3.

Namaste.

# COUNTY FERMANAGH

Many have tried to describe the lost world of Fermanagh. Fermanagh is essentially unknowable, due to the impenetrable walls built up in the hearts and minds of the local people. Ancient mystics argue that Fermanagh will never win an All-Ireland because half of Fermanagh is farmland and the other half belongs to the Queen.

# Top five things you don't want to miss:

### 1. The Muck Truck
Join the locals in their weekly pilgrimage to the Muck Truck once the pubs close. The Muck Truck is the only place to eat dinner in Fermanagh. Everywhere else, people just seem to be throwing muck at each other.

### 2. The Diamond
This is the control centre of Fermanagh. The Diamond is an outdoor adult play centre of drunken social breeding. The Diamond isn't really a diamond, it's really more of a healing crystal you'd buy on Wish.com.

### 3. Talking to a local about how *Game of Thrones* was filmed here to watch their eyes gloss over.
*Game of Thrones*? No one in Fermanagh owns their own television.

### 4. Come for the culture, stay for the floods!
Fermanagh is more watery than your drunk granny's gravy. It floods here every nine minutes. The Fermanaghians have developed a thick skin due to the torrential weather. They just accept that the river might run its course and their home will be in a different location when they wake up.

### 5. Stairway to Heaven
This is a great place to go if you love observing TikTok people trying to pimp out natural scenery for likes and comments on social media. The stairs are so rickety they say the Stairway to Heaven was built by a plumber. Which would explain why there's never any plumbers available to stop the floods. The Stairway to Heaven takes so long you'll wish the heavens would open up and put you out of your misery.

**TOXICITY RATING: 9.6**

# Enniskillen

Enniskillen is the biggest town in the lost world of Fermanagh. It's the only island town in Ireland. Which sounds impressive, until you find out Enniskillen is just called an island town because if you try to escape, one of the local gatekeepers will throw you into the surrounding river.

## Urban myths and legends

This town is controlled by Willie Boyd. Willie is a political agitator who interrupted a television broadcast in the town a few years ago. The Enniskillians saw Willie as a hero after this disruption. The Karl Marx of the Northern countryside. There is a statue erected in Willie's honour, but because you can only see it if you really believe it's there, it's actually invisible.

Asda reigns supreme over the realm of Enniskillen. This is a foothold of Enniskillian culture, the low prices and quality produce creates a very unsettling effect. It causes people from Cavan to make the pilgrimage up here once a month to do their shopping. It's possible to spot a Cavanite out from the crowd without even speaking to them. They'll be the ones arguing with the ticket inspector over the price of a train fare. Which is why they didn't pay.

The people of Enniskillen have not been the same since Wetherspoons shut down. Out of respect for this national institution, the locals still make reference to it as a sign of solidarity. They say 'I'll meet ye outside the Wetherspoons at two, chat to ye after.' The locals are living in the delusion that Wetherspoons isn't shut down. It is a protective measure they must take to stop them from realising the harrowing truth that Fermanagh is really just Laois, but with Protestants. The land of Enniskillen is divided. Divided between Catholic households and households that are under-water due to the constant flooding.

## *NIGHTLIFE*

Blakes is one of the oldest pubs in Ireland. There's a real homely atmosphere in here. They even have their own private rooms you can bring your entire family into where you can start arguing with each other to make you feel at home and simulate your natural habitat. It's reported that many have tried to come here for a quick pint and have stayed until last orders, because the seats have a special technology that makes you so relaxed that the thought of leaving the pub is terrifying. So be warned, if you go to Blakes, you might like it so much that you end up moving to Fermanagh, which is, obviously, insane.

Namaste.

# COUNTY GALWAY

Galway is the septic scab in the world of spirituality. It's full of buskers and crusties. The busker and the crustie are not mutually exclusive. One can be both a busker and a crustie at the same time. This breed of humanoid are known as cruskers. You can spot them because they'll have dreadlocks and stink of weed. They can be found hanging around Eyre Square playing the bongos and losing their train of thought mid-sentence. Deeper into the Galwegian countryside, you'll find hurlers, farmers and girls in county jerseys. These three archetypes may seem slightly different from each other, although when they drink enough Buckfast, they all morph into one.

# Top five things you don't want to miss:

### 1. Supermac's

Tell someone from Galway you don't like Supermac's. Galwegians are generally an easy-going bunch. But if you so much as hint at the possibility that Supermac's isn't the centre of the universe, they will strike you down with a vengeance as vicious as it is unexpected.

### 2. The Spanish Arch

Down a bottle of tonic wine and smoke a joint of dodgy hash under the arch to see things through the eyes of a Galwegian. And then get violently sick.

### 3. Quay Street

Walk down Quay Street and try not to bump into someone you haven't spoken to in ten years. Try it! It's impossible. Quay Street is where you're guaranteed to walk right into someone you've completely forgotten about because their existence neither adds nor takes away any value from your life.

### 4. Trying to have a normal conversation with someone from Connemara

This is a great activity for people who like a challenge! Connemara people are made up of a diet of hard-boiled eggs and repressed emotions. They have defensive walls built up that stop you from getting to know them; they even speak in Irish to ensure you don't have a clue what they're saying about you.

### 5. Visiting Salthill

Leave a Dryrobe on the ground and watch the locals fight over it like it's the last vessel to leave the *Titanic*.

**TOXICITY RATING: 9.2**

# Galway City

Galway was invented by Supermac's back in the '80s. Galwegians are genetically encoded to view Supermac's as their primary caregiver. Because people from Galway don't have parents. They just have immature adults who made a drunken mistake during rag week. Galwegians always seem to brag about Supermac's as if they built it themselves. Whenever Galwegians leave Galway they inevitably don't know what to do with themselves, so they congregate at the nearest Supermac's at the end of every night out for safety and warmth. There's a small minority of Galway natives who secretly think Supermac's is gross . . . but you'll never hear from them. Because Galway made sure they were silenced, usually on the street outside Supermac's at 3 a.m., with a drunken flurry of flying fists.

Galway is famously known as the death of ambition, because this is where hopeful Leaving Cert students go to drop out of college and take yokes. Galway is home to visitors who forgot to leave. In fact, no one from Galway is from Galway, except the people who are from Galway, they're all from Galway. Despite the high levels of traffic, no one in Galway is ever going anywhere. Once you reach the most westerly part of Galway you end up back in Eyre Square, listening to shit buskers, wondering what sort of brain trauma makes people want to listen to someone with dreadlocks play 'Hotel California' on a ukulele.

The east side of Galway is a barren wasteland, and when the people of the east can afford the bus fare into the city, they migrate in their droves to ruin everyone's night. Everyone thinks Salthill is a wealthy village but it's really just a gigantic coffee kiosk. If the prom wasn't there it would just be Mayo with a makeover. Rich Galway people don't have an accent, because there are no rich people in Galway. Just people who think a Bichon Frisé is a fashion statement rather than a sentient life form.

## Urban myths and legends

Spanish Arch, also known as Sparch, which is the sound a dying pigeon makes, is the centre of the Galwegian social life. It's powered entirely on the energy of the nearest off-licence. Sparch overlooks the River Corrib, the only river in Ireland made entirely out of Buckfast. This is the main place in Galway where privileged college students get to directly interface with the Galway 'sublas', the boy racers and the 'mongs' in real time . . . Subla is the Galwegian term for 'yup bro'. The cap-sporting, Claddaghwearing sublas are a dangerous bunch when they're under the influence of thinking they're hard.

The boy racer is a close relation to the subla. The boy racer is just a subla with a car. The boy racers still seem to think it's 1997, if the reg plate on their Honda civic is to be believed. Never underestimate the political power of the boy racers. They congest the traffic flow in Galway every week with their mass gathering of Salthill Sundays, where they listen to the Vengaboys on a dodgy speaker and Bluetooth each other fighting videos on their Sony Ericssons.

Right next to the subla, you have the mong. Although still in the same family, the mong doesn't garner any respect from the subla or the boy racer, let alone from himself. The mong can upgrade his social status to subla or boy racer through an initiation phase of downing a bottle of Buckfast in front of them without getting sick. There's a six-month probationary period once the Galwegian evolves from being a mong to a subla, in which he can revert back to being a mong if he mentions acoustic gigs in the Róisín Dubh, craft beer or NUIG.

Another subset of the Spanish Arch colony is the Galway huns. These are girls between the ages of 16–27 who wear oversized Galway jerseys and a clownish amount of make-up. All they talk about is what happened at the Galway races. The difference between Galway huns from the town and rural Galway huns is that the town girls listen to Ariana Grande, while the rural girls think Ariana Grande is the name of a hipster cappuccino that you'd never find in Ballinasloe.

Spanish Arch was closed for a few months because everyone was enjoying themselves a bit too much, and the Gardaí were getting too much enjoyment out of stealing their cans.

Galwegians' overuse of the word 'sham' is a distraction to hide their poor grasp of the English language, seeing as Galway is pretty much a giant Gaeltacht. For anyone who never got to enjoy the Gaeltacht experience, it's where teenagers go to learn how to drink, be uncomfortable around the opposite sex and acclimatise themselves to enjoying the shit music they hear at the junior disco to prepare themselves for a lifetime of hanging around in Copper's.

The crusties of Galway are a breed of white, dreadlocked wannabe-Rastafarians from Connemara who all congregate to play the bongo, get stoned and walk their dog on a rope for a leash. Ironically, they can be found gathered together on Shop Street, even though they don't believe in money. Although these crusties seem approachable, be warned. They will try to rip you off if you buy weed off them, because deep down, even more than they love the peace-loving lifestyle, they love fucking someone over with a good scam.

There are so many hen nights on in Galway that the council actually made it illegal for these loud women to stay in hotels. Instead, they built chicken coops so they would have a safe, soundproof environment to drink in without wrecking everyone's head.

Galwegians, can you please stop calling Galway G-town? You're from Connemara, not Colorado. Galwegians, we've got to take a stand against the artists and people trying to make Galway a better place. Just leave Galway alone, it's fine. Let's rebel against the powers that want to turn Karma Alley into a coffee shop. Keep Galway out of top ten lists in the Journal.ie! Together we can stop Galway from becoming a health-conscious food truck.

Namaste.

## Ballinasloe

Ballinasloe is a town in the East of Galway. It holds a significant place in Irish history, as it acts as a buffer to protect Galway from the natives of Mayo. Ballinasloe people don't generally associate with either Galway or Mayo. They only trust other people from Ballinasloe. They even leave their doors wide open at night. Nobody ever dares rob a house in the ecosystem of Ballinasloe. Although Ballinasloe may not be bound down by the laws and ethics that govern the rest of the country, they have developed their own set of morals and beliefs that keep them from causing harm to others. This is due to the magical powers indigenous to the area that turn you into a horse if you step out of line and also because everyone in Ballinasloe is always only two metres away from a loaded shotgun. This is usually in a locked press in the kitchen beside a statue of the Virgin Mary or various other Ballinasloe-approved religious memorabilia.

### What you'll find here

Ballinasloe has more Supermac's per capita than any other part of the country.  Everyone who lives there is legally obliged to eat chilli cheese chips at least three times a day. Upon entering Ballinasloe, everyone, regardless of age, race or gender has to sign an agreement stating that when they leave Ballinasloe they're only allowed talk about two things: Supermac's and Ballinasloe. Did you know? Supermac's at night time becomes Ballinasloe's only ice-skating rink. The staff throw all the ice from the machine on the ground and mixes it with Fairy Liquid. This crystallises the floor and turns it into an indestructible mound of glaciers that are perfect for skating on. You can only travel into this ice-skating rink through astral projection in your mind's eye because the doors are locked and it's not an ice-skating rink in real life.

The October Fair is held in Ballinasloe every year and it's the oldest horse fair in Europe. This is a much-feared event by the natives of Ballinasloe because without fail every year the horses become sentient and sell their owners to other horses. The horses make the owners dress up in really nice clothes to make them look more expensive. But instead, the sadness on their faces makes them look like they just got dressed up by a horse. The October Fair is a bad place to go if you wouldn't like to be auctioned off by a horse, but it's a great place to go if you believe in equality for all horses and think it's time for restitution. Horstitution.

Another strangely mystical quality of Ballinasloe is the famous 'lazy wall' on the main street. This wall got its name because if you sit down on it for too long a flagon of cider magically appears in your hand and all of a sudden you find you're still sitting in the same place five years later. Nobody you love will talk to you anymore.

## NIGHTLIFE

The hive mind of Ballinasloe yearns for its much-missed nightclub to re-open. The Planet was the social hub of the native people of Ballinasloe, who loved listening to Tiësto tracks while drinking Beamish and not talking too much. The nightclub shut down because it was colonised by horses during the fair and turned into a stable. The nightclub owners were totally against the idea but there were so many horses in there that they didn't have a say in the matter. The colonisation of the Planet by horses meant that there was a consistent smell of hay in the club that the staff refused to explain to the punters, in case the horses killed them.

Namaste.

# COUNTY KERRY

People in Kerry like to think they live in a kingdom. But the only thing that they have in common with the royal family is that most of them have had a sexual relationship with at least one of their cousins. Which isn't actually that bad, because everyone in Kerry is related to each other anyway. The locals here think being from Kerry is a personality type. They say this makes them like people from Cork, just with about 15 per cent less aggression.

# Top five things you don't want to miss:

## 1. Kerryisms

It can be very difficult to understand what Kerry folk are saying, because they have so many obscure catchphrases you'll be convinced they're just making them up as they go along. A word of warning: never question them on the meaning of the catchphrase: this will arouse hostility. Just laugh along and hope for the best while slowly backing away from them and moving towards the nearest exit.

## 2. Asking a local why does everyone keep talking about Sam Maguire like you're supposed to know who that is?

A classic. For bonus points, look a Tralee native dead in the eyes after the Sunday game and ask them if Sam Maguire is a good plumber.

## 3. The King Puck fair

In the kingdom, even the goats wear crowns. If you'd like to see a ceremony where a group of townspeople huddle around a bejewelled farm animal, come on down to Killorglin on 10 August.

## 4. Covering yourself in Kerry Gold and standing out in a field

Watch as the locals crowd around you like a flock of mosquitos on a fresh carcass.

## 5. The Ring of Kerry

Not the scenic drive, the Ring of Kerry is a never-ending cycle that Kerry natives find themselves trapped in where they have to tone down their incessant talk about Kerry when they are working in Dublin. This can often lead to what is known as a Kerry relapse, where the Kerry native will explode and just keep shouting 'Kerry bah' over and over until their lungs are red raw from screaming, or someone hits them and steals their Nokia 3310, which is the only phone people from Kerry know how to use.

## TOXICITY RATING: 9.7

# Tralee

Tralee is a town in County Kerry. Tralee has by far the biggest population of any town in the county. It's similar to a hollowed-out giant marshmallow. It's so big and soft and empty on the inside. Tralee is a great destination to choose if you want people to stare at you from afar as you walk into the area wearing Doc Martens and a leather jacket. It's also a great destination to run away from if you like being chased with a pitchfork. Despite all that can be said about Tralee, it has many redeeming qualities: here are some of them.

## What you'll find here

If you take a walk into Tralee town square on a rainy day the square actually turns into an ice rink. The square was recently voted the most dangerous place in Ireland. The locals all play a game where they try not to slip and fall to their death. Sometimes they win! Whenever this game takes place, an Irish country-rock wedding band play music really loudly until the Gardaí escort them on. Which never happens, because the Gardaí in Tralee are usually in the pub. As a result, this game has been on-going for about sixteen years. The people of Tralee barely notice it happening anymore.

The Rose of Tralee is the main cash cow of the town. It's been going for centuries, some say before roses were even invented. The myth goes that this show has always been about a perception of beauty and pride. The show is really just a token event to give people an excuse to flock to the town park afterwards, where all the population of Tralee were conceived.

The Abrakebabra in Tralee is invisible. It's the closest Kerry will ever get to being magic. It only appears after a Debs takes place in the town, when it becomes the busiest place in the world. When you step inside the Abrakebabra realm, you will find a hidden tunnel in the back that stretches all the way to Killarney. No one ever dares travel that far. If word got out that there was a secret passageway to a chain restaurant in Killarney they'd burn the place to the ground.

The Daily Grind is where the hipsters of Tralee feel safe. It's famous for having the best coffee in the town. It's also famous for being the only place that isn't a pub that serves coffee in town. The Daily Grind is an open, friendly environment, provided you have a handlebar moustache and are typing up a novella that will never get published on your unbranded laptop.

## NIGHTLIFE

Hennessy's is the central location of Tralee late-night drinking. It's the favourite place of people who like ordering fancy cocktails called 'Sour Daithi'. Many people have been curious, who is Daithi? But we'll never find out, because he's barred. Hennessy's is known for its versatility. It's the only place in the world you'll find a combination of high-end mixed drinks and loud men who look like they're on day three of a wedding celebration shouting in the DJ's ear to play 'Don't Look Back in Anger'.

Horan's was a renowned nightclub in Tralee. Like all the great things in Tralee, it closed recently due to circumstances beyond human control. In other words, people from Cork City began to infiltrate and they had to shut the place down immediately. Horan's used to have the most highly advanced technology in all of Kerry. The bouncers there had an almost robotic intelligence that allowed them to spot fake IDs from approximately a mile away. They then launched unruly underage drinkers into a cannon, sending them into Limerick to let them be feasted upon by a pack of wild hyenas.

The natives of Tralee pine for Fabric nightclub. It is the oldest nightclub in Kerry and has reopened and closed more times than a broken door in the wind. It's believed the fingerprints of Michael Collins can be found on the rail of the bar, due to him clutching onto it tightly when a bouncer reefed him out for smoking indoors. Fabric underwent the ancient cycle of all Tralee nightclubs: Fabric – shut down, reopened and renamed Quarters, shut down – now it's a gym. The health-conscious movement of Tralee have been undermining everything worthwhile in the town. Trying to shut down everywhere that people experience enjoyment, one bar at a time. The Tralee natives someday will rise against the healthy living movement and decide to stop exercising and going for ten-kilometre runs, opting instead to drink themselves into a stupor from the comfort of their own homes.

Namaste.

# Dingle town

Dingle is the only town on the Dingle peninsula, or the 'Dingle peninch' as self-obsessed, positive-mindset ex-rugby lads from the Southside of Dublin probably call it when they're trying to sound exotic. Dingle is a resting place for the souls of holiday-goers who got bored to death after deciding it might be fun to go to a pub and listen to someone play a bodhrán all night. Dingle is a Mecca for Irish music. They even lock self-identified Irish Americans in cages and make them watch clips of Des Bishop over and over again until they experience sadness.

## Urban myths and legends

Dingle is famously known as a fishing port. When visiting Dingle, make sure to catch a glimpse of your bloated reflection in the glistening Atlantic Ocean. Sadists from far and wide used to make the pilgrimage down to Dingle every summer to try to fish Fungie the Dolphin out of the water so they could cook him alive and eat him. Animal rights activists were also looking to cook and eat Fungie, to protect him from the sadists who want to cook him and eat him, which would obviously be much worse. Everyone knows, if you're going to get cooked and eaten it may as well be from the knives and forks of people that love you. More recent reports suggest that Fungie might be missing, or worse, presumed dead. This should come as no surprise, seeing as there were queues of people hunting him down so they could cook him and eat him.

## Local cuisine

Experience the gastro-intestinal cuisine of Dingle. This is a haven for foodies. Foodies is another word for people who swapped any interesting aspects of their personality for a slice of avocado toast on wholewheat bread and a blog that no one reads. Foodies usually flock in groups. But they are groups of people that secretly hate each other. Foodies can't be friends with other foodies, they are too judgemental to let other people exist in their universe, unless they compliment them about their blog – which, obviously, no one does. There are over fifty restaurants in Dingle, with a population of only 2,000 that means the restaurants could technically fit everyone in Dingle all the time, leaving their houses empty for squatters to invade.

Dingle is famously a Gaeltacht town, which makes tourists think they're in a different country, like Norway, or Cork. Dingle is a relic of an Ireland that most of the country has left in the past. Sometimes the locals speak in Irish around unrecognised outsiders just so they can secretly talk about their plan to cook and eat Fungie.

## NIGHTLIFE

Dick Mack's is the place to go if you love drinking whiskey and pretending the hangover doesn't make you cry. The friendly staff and spacious outdoor area make for a great atmosphere to get so drunk that you forget you're in Kerry. It's rumoured that after the fourth glass of whiskey, the air in Dingle changes and Micheal Ó Muircheartaigh starts commenting all the greatest mistakes of your life over and over in your head until you fall asleep from the stress and shit yourself.

Namaste.

## Ballyheigue

Ballyheigue is a coastal village in the north of Kerry. It's famous for its extraordinary views of the ocean and drunk, friendly old men shouting at you in accents you won't be able to understand. Ballyheigue natives always chat over the wall to their neighbours in Tralee, even though they're 18 km away from each other, because people from Kerry have really loud voices.

### Urban myths and legends

The natives of Ballyheigue will be quick to tell you no trip to Ballyheigue is complete without visiting Ballyheigue Castle, despite the fact that the castle got burnt to the ground by the IRA during the War of Independence a hundred years ago. The remains of the castle now serve as a visual buffer that obstructs the path of a nine-hole golf course that was built by descendants of the British landlords who built the castle in the first place. Rumours suggest that this castle is a hub of paranormal activity. Just the original. All of the remakes were shit.

Ballyheigue is famous for its monastic sites. Most notably, a well by the name of 'Tobar na Súl', which roughly translates to 'the well for the eyes'. Gullible people flock here every year to try to heal their visual impairments, but all they end up doing is getting their faces wet and bumping into things. There's a gift shop at the exit of the well that sells invisible socks that would say *I love Kerry* if you were able to read them.

They say if you flock to the mountains of Dingle late at night a dog will follow you around with a pack of biscuits strapped to his back in case you get hungry and need a snack to maintain sustenance on your treacherous journey. Years will pass and you will regale your family with tales about a dog that followed you around in the dead of the night with human treats strapped to his back and they'll only smile in hidden undertones of disbelief, fearing for your sanity.

The sand dunes behind the beach of Ballyheigue are a den of youthful drinking and smoking. This is where young adults try to relive the nostalgia of their teenage years by going down and buying four cans of Karpackie and a block of soapbar they nicked off their weird uncle who smells like a mixture of stolen communion money and sandalwood.

Ballyheigue hosts a week-long summer festival every year, which the entire population of Kerry, Cork and Limerick call in sick to attend. Some of these people lost their jobs once their bosses saw them putting up pictures in their swimming togs going for a swim with the caption hashtagged #blessed #ballyheiguesummerfestival #fuckyoubossimnotreallysick. This festival has something for everyone: wine-tasting for the adults, face-painting for the kids; they even have a pig-racing event. Which is where they'll pull two locals off their barstools in Reagan's and make them race each other while someone runs behind them with a hot iron rod.

## NIGHTLIFE

The nightlife in Ballyheigue only exists for three months in the summer. On 1 September the electricity in Ballyheigue goes off and the entire village is engulfed in darkness. The locals are cryogenically frozen for nine months until the first settlers from Cork arrive on their summer holidays the following year. Jimmy Browne's is one of the favourite watering holes of both locals and tourists alike. It's reported this pub has the creamiest pint of Guinness on this side of the Kerry border. At first glance it seems like a cosy traditional Irish pub, but all the locals there are really just extras in a horror film that never got funded, they all got shipped off to Ballyheigue and told to do an impression of what it means to be quintessentially Irish. They have the most convincing accents, you'd almost swear they weren't homesick British drama school graduates.

Namaste.

# COUNTY KILDARE

Kildare is a mystery. Half of the locals here base their entire personality around the fact that they're not from Dublin even though they think they are just because they constantly go there on a bus. The other half are horse people with neutral accents and a crippling gambling addiction. They say in Kildare there are more stud farms than there are lads with eyebrow slits who think they're hard. And that's saying something because there's thousands of them.

# Top five things you don't want to miss:

## 1. Punchestown festival
This is a favourite spot of the Kildare natives. In fact, they are nocturnal creatures who only wake up when the races are on. For the rest of the year they lie in a sleep pod and dream of being chased around Kildare town by Ray D'Arcy.

## 2. Kildare Village
Kildare Village is a human zoo. It's where the Canada Goose yupbros, white fluffy dog-walking yummy mummies and confused tourists merge as one. Make sure to take a visit and eat an overpriced crêpe in the rain.

## 3. Bringing up the death of the 66 bus
The 66 bus was the only thing people in Kildare could ever talk about. When the 66 route was axed it killed the Kildare spirit. So people in Kildare no longer leave their homes.

## 4. Watching Confey and Leixlip fight for the approval of Naas
Go to any of the local nightclubs in Kildare to watch Leixlip and Confey fight like two abandoned children for the praise of Naas, their distant and loveless father.

## 5. The M50 into Dublin

**TOXICITY RATING: 8.8**

# Leixlip

People from Leixlip dress like they live in Dublin, and people from Dublin think Leixlip is the name of some weird dressing you'd never order on a salad.

Leixlip was a well-known Viking town, and some 500 years later they got colonised again by Intel in the late '90s. Intel didn't want the truth leaking to the press, so to stop news spreading to social media, the only type of phone you can get here is a Tesco mobile and everyone here still uses dial-up to connect to the internet. So I can say whatever I want, because no one from Leixlip will ever see this.

## Urban myths and legends

Despite the deadening grip of the colonial overlords, Leixlip has forever been in a state of civil unrest. Leixlip is separated into two warring factions: the hillers and the farenders. The hillers and the farenders have been engaging in a war so barbaric it makes neighbouring areas of Maynooth and Celbridge want to hide in the safe hands of Lucan.

The first thing you notice in Leixlip is the horrible stench coming from the River Rye. It's not the river's fault, Leixlip doesn't have any running water, so this is where the locals all wash themselves, and people from Leixlip naturally smell like dirty river water.

One of the main attractions in Leixlip is a structure known as the wonderful barn, which is neither a barn nor is it wonderful ... Nobody knows what it does or why it's here. but it does look like a giant stone ice cream cone that fell out of the sky. The wonderful barn is well known as the safe place where Irish youngsters go to taste their formative sip of chronic alcoholism.

Confey is a small suburb of Leixlip, because Leixlip actually has subsections if you can believe that. All Confey is known for is having a SuperValu and a GAA club, yet they still want to gain independence from the rest of Leixlip so that they can become Leixlip 2.0, which is just Leixlip with fewer people in it.

Due to Leixlip bordering Kildare and Dublin, in the fifteenth century it was the outpost for the Pale. The Pale was the strip of land in Ireland that was the base for English rule. Out of this came the phrase we now know as 'beyond the Pale' – a blanket term that describes everywhere outside the Bermuda triangle of the Dublin–Meath–Kildare border. It was also used in tribute to the Leixlip natives' pale complexion. It's reported that when a family from Leixlip goes on an all-inclusive holiday in the sun, all they come back with is a headache.

Another interesting facet of life in Leixlip is that Leixlip has two train stations: one for the hillers and the other for the farenders, but the trains only arrive every hour, and no one from Leixlip ever leaves Leixlip. So it's really just for decoration.

### NIGHTLIFE

The best pub in Leixlip is the Salmon Leap, and the main advantage of this Leixlip bar is the fact that it's actually in Lucan.

Something happened to the hiller and farender youths once they turned eighteen and started going to the Ozone nightclub. Through the process of socialisation in the smoking area, they put their small differences aside to show solidarity against the global superpower that has kept them divided for all these years. Yes, still Intel. But somewhere in their slurred singleness of purpose they got sidetracked, so instead of protesting against Intel they just went to Sam's chipper. The consumer capitalist economy saw that Ozone was a threat so they knocked it down and replaced it with an Aldi. This was the final beat of the butterfly's wings, rural Ireland's death knell. The mouth of this town is bleeding, corporate interests bit her on the Leixlip.

Namaste.

## Naas

Naas is a fantastic holiday destination for people who hate themselves. Naas in Irish means 'assembly'. Which is fitting, because much like the school kids who had to go to this weekly depressive event, nobody wants to be here either. Whenever someone says they're from Naas, everyone assumes they live on the side of a motorway, because they do. Naas is mostly famous for the Naas ball, which is a big circular structure on the side of the main road. Nobody has a clue why it's there. Studies have revealed that the purpose for this spherical monstrosity is two-fold. To the people living in Naas, it is a sign that they're nearly home and to the people visiting Naas, it's a sign that they should turn back, because they're nearly in Naas and there's still time to reconsider. Rumours have been circulating about the Naas ball since time began. Some say the government hollowed out the ball with all the discontinued Nokia phones once the iPhone came on the market. At that point, science hadn't developed enough for the phones to be disposed of, which is why they had to hide them in the Naas ball instead. Nokias are virtually indestructible.

## What you'll find here

In the greater Naas area there are three major racecourses: Punchestown, the Curragh and Naas racecourse. This is so that enthusiastic gamblers can convince themselves that no one knows how many times they've put the house on it and lost. The people of the racecourses are an interesting bunch. The time capsule of the racecourses makes people age in reverse, which means the lads in their 20s wearing farmers' caps are in their 60s, and the lads in their 60s wearing farmers' caps are on Tik Tok. The racecourse also contains disinterested women in elegant dresses who just nod their heads every few minutes to let you know that they're still awake. It's impossible to decipher the language of the racecourse people due to their unrecognisably strong country accents. It's believed that once a local sets foot on the racecourse they start speaking in tongues and jiving to Irish country music.

The Naas GAA club is the focal point of Naas culture. This is home to Gaelic football, hurling and roaring Kildarean mothers who strike fear into the hearts of referees for simply doing their job.

Naas town centre is the shopping district in Naas. There's really something for everyone here. There is a Costa coffee shop for people who want to bring their laptop around with them in public and pretend they're writing a book. There's a Holland & Barrett here, for those who like to portray the illusion of health and wellness. Last but not least there's also a float lab here, for people who like to listen to Joe Rogan and pretend to be comfortable with the deafening silence of their innermost thoughts.

The natives of Naas seek refuge along the canal, where they drink cans on a sunny day. If these local folk tilt their head to a 45-degree angle and squint their eyes slightly, for a few moments they can forget they're in Kildare and pretend they're in France.

## NIGHTLIFE

The best nightclub in Naas can be found upstairs at the Naas Court Hotel, but only because there's just one nightclub in Naas. This hotel is also an excellent destination to rest your head if you like falling asleep to the background noise of drunken late-night revelling uncles singing rebel songs in the smoking area.

The social life of Naas is a unique phenomenom. Due to the high levels of Catholic guilt endemic to the people of Naas, the pubs in the area are segregated by gender. The young women of Naas go to McCormacks Pub, fondly known as 'Macks'. The young men go to Fletcher's. When the pubs close, the young men and women of Naas evacuate the dancefloor and meet up at the benches outside Abrakebabra. Due to the lack of socialisation, the males and females don't know how to interact with each other. They inevitably end up talking about how much they hate people from Celbridge.

Despite the growing pains of becoming fully evolved human beings, all progress will be wiped away soon. The government decided to plant a Wetherspoons in Naas. This is a concealed effort at urban sprawl to raise the rent prices in Naas and make it seem like it's a landing strip for listless influencers who are yet to make an influence on anything or anyone.

Namaste.

## Celbridge

Celbridge is a bustling town on the border of Kildare and Dublin. Much like the Republicans up North who are more Irish than the Irish, the Kildare natives of Celbridge are more Dublin than a spice burger and a loud argument. Many famous people are from Celbridge. Most notably, Arthur Guinness. Arthur isn't his real name. His parents thought his head was shaped like a pint glass. When Arthur was born they decided to call him Baby Guinness.

## Urban myths and legends

Due to the infrastructure put in place over the last few years, Celbridge has become a town on the commuter belt of Dublin. As a result, barely anyone from Celbridge is from Kildare. Even the Celbridgeans native to County Kildare have Dublin accents. Although if you throw a rock in a south-westerly direction, it'll hit someone over the head in the neighbouring region of Straffan, causing them to yelp in a thick Kildare accent. People from Kildare never speak, they only make involuntary sounds when they are in pain or amused. This is why no one really knows what the Kildare accent sounds like.

Celbridge and Leixlip have been fighting over which town is closer to Dublin, as both border the county. It's obvious that Leixlip is the winner, geographically speaking. Celbridge just loves to get into arguments. There are a small subsection of Celbridge that don't really care where they are but you never hear from them because the government of Celbridge removed their vocal cords.

The Celbridge forest is a magical wonderland of naggin-induced bliss. This is where most natives of Celbridge discover who they really are, often while getting sick into a bush due to alcohol poisoning. Some of these young Celbridgeans end up growing up, leaving the forest and graduating to Maynooth University. Others end up graduating from day-drinking to night-time raving in the forest. Unable to see the wood for the trees due to the amount of ketamine they've consumed.

Celbridgeans are incredibly nostalgic about their past. They have great loyalty to their town. They even still call the local shop 'Vivo' because that's what it was called before Daybreak took over and turned it into a franchise. The Celbridge locals love the word 'Vivo' 'because it has far fewer letters than 'Daybreak' and it rhymes with Bebo, the only social media platform people from Celbridge are still on.

### NIGHTLIFE

This phenomenon can also be observed in the local pub. Celbridgeans know it as 'Celbridge House' even though it got re-named 'The Henry Grattan' a few years ago. The natives refuse to call this pub by its new name for two reasons. Firstly: it's too close to the bone. Henry Grattan was an Irish politician who fought for the rights of the Irish from Westminster and failed, much like how people from Celbridge fight for the right of pretending to be from Dublin and fail. Secondly, because Celbridgeans have a devastating fear of change.

Namaste.

# Nurney

Suprisingly, there are two places called Nurney in Ireland. I haven't heard of either of them. Here we are discussing Nurney in County Kildare. The other Nurney is in County Carlow. Allegedly the distance between the schools in each Nurney is precisely the length of a marathon, 26.2 miles. Which is great news for the parents of the local students, seeing as all there is to do in Nurney is exercise.

## Urban myths and legends

Much like the mystical Fingal County, many road-users are familiar with Nurney from signposts alone. It's on the same exit as Kildare Village on the motorway. The people of Nurney feel a great pride about their hidden utopia, shying away beneath the sprawling shadow of consumer culture. Nurney is a place that exists for most as a concept of the mind. Usually followed by the realisation that there's never much of a need to go there.

## What you'll find here

Nurney used to have two shops in it but Spar swallowed it up and now reigns supreme on the isolated throne of Nurney groceries. Nurney is one of the few places in Ireland that has one shop and two graveyards. If you walk around Nurney after O'Brien's pub closes and roll a cigarette, a portal into a parallel dimension opens up. You end up in a magical place called Nurnia. It's just Nurney but everyone has eyebrows on their shoulders and legs on their chest. They keep frantically asking you what time it is because everyone in Nurnia is eternally late for the most important meeting of their lives. Nurnia is Nurney with unneccesary New York energy.

## NIGHTLIFE

O'Brien's pub is the local watering hole of the Nurney natives. It's a quiet place with friendly staff who always go above and beyond to make their customers happy. They'll even sing a rendition of 'Happy Birthday' if you ask them to, even if it's not your birthday and you don't ask them to. *Especially* if it's not your birthday. The staff here are optimists, they know it's bound to be someday this year. The people of Nurney are a humble lot. They'd never tell you themselves but some of the best pool players come from this little village. All due to the fact that O'Brien's has a pool table. This has made everyone in Nurney adept at the ancient art of knocking balls into holes for money.

Namaste.

# Sallins

Sallins is a small town in Kildare. It's situated along the Grand Canal. This gives the locals an hour's respite from their quiet life of waiting around until it's time to go on a walk along the Grand Canal, which is all there really is to do in Sallins. Sallins is an escape route for those that are sick of having a hectic schedule. This is why people move here from Dublin and ruin the ambience by being too loud and jumping in the canal whenever the sun comes out in February.

## What you'll find here

When visiting Sallins, make sure to check out the abandoned mill in the centre of the town. It used to be an Odlum's mill before it was shut down. It was the main source of employment in Sallins, but unfortunately, they had to shut their doors forever once the government found out they were turning people into owls. Eventually, over 30 per cent of the workforce were owls and kept showing up late because they slept all day and hunted all night. The closure of this staple of the Sallins lifestyle led to the locals having to commute further afield to seek out employment.

Once you take a stroll through the streets of Sallins, you can't help but notice this place lives in the shadow of its colonial oppressors, Naas. Naas is the golden child of the Kildare family, while Sallins basks in the darkness waiting for another factory to open. When the young adults of Sallins talk about emigration, they're not talking about Australia or Canada, they're talking about finally taking the plunge and moving all the way out to Naas. Some have made the excursion over the years. Once a Sallins local moves to Naas they have to disconnect from their entire family and any friends from Sallins, while also being required to sleep in a poorly fitted three-piece suit that they bought on DoneDeal off a stranger whose home smells like dust.

Sallins is embedded with a rich local history. One such event was the Sallins train robbery of 1976. Bandits burgled the Cork-to-Dublin mail train, making off with 200,000 Irish pounds, the equivalent to 1.1 million euro today. There was never any hard evidence about who committed the crime at the time, although the perpetrators went on record to admit it years later. The judge ignored the admission and decided to place the blame on the first three lads he saw hanging around outside the chipper wearing Celtic jerseys.

## NIGHTLIFE

The main den of activity lies in a desolate landscape known as 'The Wastelands' where the outdoor drinkers of Sallins commune and watch their dreams vanish into dust to the soundtrack of 'Adagio for Strings' on a half-broken portable speaker. Many have charted this treacherous environment to find lads from Newbridge commandeering the vicinity with their greased mullets and the overpowering odour of Lynx Chocolate laying waste to the olfactory senses.

Namaste.

# Athy

Athy is an up-and-coming market town in Kildare. A geographical personality split exists here, rural and urban. The stretching green fields cast long shadows in the summer, shadows from the exhausted bodies of wage workers who got outpriced from the city and have to drive to Dublin every morning on a donkey's back. Athy is known for its cultural heritage, which is what every town in Ireland says about itself when they don't have their own beach. One thing to note when visiting Athy is the heavy traffic. If you try getting out of Athy during working hours it's nearly impossible, because everyone in Athy sleeps in their car and waits until it's time to commute to Dublin.

## Urban myths and legends

Crom Abu bridge is the walkway above the River Barrow that stops the locals from accidentally falling into the water and drowning because they can't swim. The bridge lies right beside White's Castle, which is a sixteenth-century tower house, originally built to guard the river. Since then the castle has been put to more resourceful use, holding anti-vaccination parties in 2021 in response to what they call the 'real virus' which is, evidently, health and safety.

When visiting Athy make sure to avail of one of the canal walks in the town. But if you do, make sure you blend in with the locals. Everyone in Athy wears Heelys. Because in Athy, it's still 2007 and nobody ever grew up. So if you don't wear Heelys, the locals will find out you're an outsider, and skate all over you.

### NIGHTLIFE

The people of Athy worship O'Brien's pub. O'Brien's isn't merely a pub, it's just being modest. O'Brien's is a multi-purpose facility. They even have a grocery at the front of the building. This is perfect for the natives of Athy. Because all they have ever wanted was to do their weekly shop, drunk.

Namaste.

# COUNTY KILKENNY

Kilkenny is a county known for being invaded by the Vikings. This is a tremendous source of pride to the Kilkennians. They even call Kilkenny a medieval stronghold. All of the old buildings the Vikings built when they came here are still standing. Which is a bit like someone who got kidnapped keeping a scrapbook of their captor. Kilkenny feel a twisted sense of joy that a fleet of blood-thirsty conquerors cared enough to colonise them.

People from Kilkenny are in a constant state of hypervigilance, always ready to jump into a conversation about how Kilkenny town is actually a city and used to be the capital of Ireland. They'll do this regardless of the context, the people present or whether or not you were talking to them in the first place.

# Top five things you don't want to miss:

### 1. Speaking badly of the hurling statue
You might think the statue looks like a man with a weapon in his hand ready to take an unprovoked swing at his next victim. But be warned: if you insult the statue, you'll offend the Kilkennians. Because if there's one thing people from Kilkenny love more than hurling, it's being viciously beaten with a stick.

### 2. Your chance to run out the exit of Kilkenny Castle
Castles are old and shit. Everyone knows it. Once you come to that realisation, you will be keen to escape at all costs.

### 3. Telling them what you really think of Smithwick's
Tell them how no one ever buys Smithwick's as a conscious choice. The only time it's socially acceptable to drink Smithwick's is at your friend's afterparty when you run out of drink. The Smithwick's always belongs to his dad, and is hidden in the utility room beside the rest of the chemical cleaning products and toxic poison, which is exactly where it belongs.

### 4. Understanding that 'Come on the cats' is nothing to do with animal porn
Even worse, it's hurling.

### 5. Talking about Tesco
Don't ever talk about Tesco to a local here. They won't have a clue who that is. Dunnes Stores (aka the Sugar Daddy of Kilkenny) bought out every single scrap of land so that Tesco couldn't set up shop here. This makes Kilkenny the only county in Ireland that doesn't have a Tesco. This is the reason why all the people here do is drink and play hurling. They have evolved to a higher level of athleticism due to the non-existent temptation of being able to buy five doughnuts for €1.50 whenever they want.

## TOXICITY RATING: 9.4

# Kilkenny City

Kilkenny is a medieval city built on the broken backs of 800 years of Irish slavery. Kilkenny fought for city status for centuries, which it finally got in 1609. But ever since the invention of GAA, all the Kilkenny natives have been able to talk about is hurling, avoiding all other forms of natural human conversations as best they could. As a result, the rest of the country has been trying to demote Kilkenny back into a town, but so far none have succeeded, because the locals use their hurls as weapons. Kilkenny was even the capital before Dublin. But now the only capital you see in Kilkenny are the capital letters that spell GET OUT OF KILKENNY WHILE YOU STILL CAN.

## Urban myths and legends

DJ Bainne is the local hero of Kilkenny. He's a milkman by day and a DJ by night. But the truth is he's not a milkman. He's just a magic DJ who has cloned himself to allow him to deliver cartons of milk and play Nathan Carter songs at the exact same time. I know this is true because you never see the milkman and the DJ in the same room together.

When visiting Kilkenny, be sure to visit Dore's nostalgia café. This is a place that serves coffees and childhood memories under the same roof. Dore has lived many lives and can bring you through a nostalgic trip of your previous existence where she was your mother and you were Napoleon, apparently. Dore is a kind woman who can not only tell you about your past, she can also predict your future. When you leave, make sure not to use a phrase like 'have a good day' because she'll say something like 'don't worry, I will; I'm going to win 150 quid on a scratch card in 20 minutes'.

### NIGHTLIFE

The Hole in the Wall – housed in the oldest surviving townhouse in Ireland – was bought by Metallica's doctor, a miracle worker who has somehow managed to keep James Hetfield alive. It's believed there's a hole in the wall of the pub that Brian Boru himself punched through when the bartender cut him off. Did you know? A Kilkenny legend has it that Brian Boru is Conor McGregor's great-great-great-grandfather.

Namaste.

# COUNTY LAOIS

The only natural reaction to Laois is: 'Sorry, who?' Laois is known for its ancient ruins. And when I say ancient ruins, obviously I mean the people. The people in Laois are older than time itself, if not in age than certainly in demeanour. The air pressure in Laois causes everyone to age in dog years. Which is why you'll see lads in their early twenties talking about turf like that's not a weird thing.

# Top five things you don't want to miss:

### 1. Reminding the locals about how Laois was known as 'the Queen's county' for about 400 years

The only time they want to hear about a bloody Mary is when they're drinking the next morning to get rid of a life-threatening hangover.

### 2. Watching someone from Offaly and Laois have a conversation with each other

Observe the friendly insults they hurl at each other in their haphazard battle for dominance. This delicate dance of territorial jousting is like watching two potholes argue over how wet the rain is. They're still potholes and not going anywhere any time soon.

### 3. Laois-based communications

Everyone in Laois is legally obliged to carry a slingshot around with them at all times. The broadband connection out here is so bad that if you're in Laois and you want to meet up with someone you have to fire a pebble at their window with a slingshot to catch their attention.

### 4. The traffic in the morning on the road to Dublin

Many Laoiseans spend the majority of their existence on the motorway to their job. This is a dangerous move. People from Laois are dangerous when they are in a car by themselves, alone with their own thoughts.

### 5. Ploughing

This is a long-held tradition in Laois. Ploughing is perhaps the most forward-thinking movement in Laois at the moment. Ploughing is a deeply cherished ritual in which a good-looking, closeted farmer goes on Grindr to blow the muck off his wellies.

**TOXICITY RATING: 9.9**

# Portarlington

Portarlington is a town in Laois surrounded by miles and miles of stretching nothingness. The Market Square in the town is the hub of the Portarlington social experience. The Market Square is the name of Portarlington's most notable bus stop. It's the only place in Portarlington where you can find people talking to each other. Usually saying something like 'When's the next bus? The app isn't working and I'm desperately trying to escape from Portarlington.'

## Urban myths and legends

Portarlington used to be called 'Portalringtown', and was once a portal that would lead you into a dimension where everything is less depressing than it is here. The universe had to shut down this portal and rename the town due to people from Portarlington throwing rocks at each other and starting fires in the new dimension.

There is a multitude of charity shops in Portarlington. Although some would see this and assume this is because people from Portarlington are generous and considerate of the less fortunate, it's really because the Portarlington natives hate paying retail prices. If there's one thing these locals won't stand for, it's charity.

There's a huge Garda station in Portarlington. This is because the Gardaí in the area requested a building with a lot of wide open space to give them room to run around and play catch with each other, but due to the lack of crime in Portarlington, it only opens for one hour every day. As a result, the Gardaí in Portarlington have the same circadian cycle as pandas: they sleep for eighteen hours a day. Allegedly they too can be found on their days off munching on bamboo sticks.

The government decided to overload Portarlington with takeaway restaurants. This was an attempt to instil a sense of indecision in the locals when trying to make an order. Pizza or a kebab? Who knows! This ensures that behind every choice made there lies a lingering feeling of eternal disappointment. Unfortunately, this has led to many people from the area starving to death.

## NIGHTLIFE

Most of the pubs in Portarlington have state-of-the-art smoking areas. This is a bid to encourage the locals to chain-smoke cigarettes in an attempt to decrease their life expectancy. These turrets of tobacco are a utopia for people who want a five-minute break from sitting on a bar stool and staring directly at the wall all night. Rhythm and Booze is one of the best-loved pubs in the area. This is mainly due to the fact that they have a Phat Burger restaurant chain attached to them. This is incredibly popular in the area, because the Portarlington natives love making a mess while drinking. Phat Burger, without explicitly saying it, have subconsciously turned this pub into a live-in facility. Many of its patrons haven't seen the light of day in centuries. This establishment has all the essentials required for a happy life: food, alcohol and a toilet. You can even wash your armpits under the sink. Namaste.

## Portlaoise

Portlaoise is the county town of Laois. The most random county in the known universe. Portlaoise is a town on the rise. It's growing up faster than the eldest child in an alcoholic home. Portlaoise, once known as the Mecca of the manufacturing industry, soon became known as the commercial epicentre of Southern Leinster, just because they have a shopping centre. The de-industrialisation of Portlaoise occurred due to the locals not wanting to work in factories anymore. Instead, most opted to work in the service sector, which is basically like being a construction worker, except that instead of physical labour you do all your work sitting down.

### Urban myths and legends

When you wander into the realm of Portlaoise, make sure to visit the Rock of Dunamase. Like most great things in Ireland, it's in ruins. The Rock of Dunamase was erected by Strongbow, before he became a cider.

Dunamase was once the seat of power of the Kings of Laois. It's now the seat of power of the lads who post 'King' in a comment under their mates' Instagram posts in Laois. This once stronghold of Irish royalty has become embroidered with cans of Strongbow, the last remaining vestige of an era once forgotten. The Rock of Dunamase overlooks the rest of Laois. Make sure to take a trip up there if you like looking at endless green fields with nowhere to hide.

Portlaoise is a Russian doll of prisons. There's the actual prison in Portlaoise, and then there's the open-air prison, which is literally every-where else in Portlaoise. Some believe the rules in the open-air prison of Portlaoise are far stricter than inside the real prison itself. It's speculated that if a native of Portlaoise spends their life not causing any trouble, they get a break from the outside world and get to go to Portlaoise prison as a reward for their good behaviour. They usually end up sharing a cell with people who are in there for innocent reasons. Like smoking weed, or arson. Arson around outside the shops bro.

## What you'll find here

A must-visit in Portlaoise is a famous piece of art known as the Blue Bridge. It no longer exists, but the locals pretend it does whenever they're giving directions to confused outsiders. You too can can simulate a sense of belonging as you join them in their collective hallucination and pretend to see a blue bridge on the Portlaoisean horizon. In their quieter moments, many natives wonder where the blue bridge went. It was discontinued in 2011 due to the efforts of a lobbyist group from Offaly who hate the colour blue, bridges and, most of all, Portlaoise.

### NIGHTLIFE

Ember is the most frequented (and only) nightclub in Portlaoise. It used to be called Egan's and was known for its homely atmosphere and friendly staff. Suddenly, Egan's became Ember and underwent a transformation, now becoming known for its chic, forward-thinking values, just because Marty Guilfoyle played here once.
Namaste.

# Stradbally

Stradbally is a small town situated in the heart of Laois. It's a ghost town for the vast majority of the year, with party-goers visiting to wreck it for a few days every summer. The locals don't seem to appreciate the influx of college students who want to take MDMA for the first time poisoning their paradise and burning the ear off them. However, they are welcomed with open arms by the local businesses, because they always seem to lick the windows clean. Stradbally is a time capsule of Irish culture where tradition and vogue intertwine to create this enclave of Midlands confusion. It's believed every time a festival-goer asks someone 'are ya havin' a good night pal?' a baby is conceived out of wedlock in Stradbally. Which in Stradbally, will get you excommunicated, because sex before marriage is still illegal.

## What you'll find here

Stradbally is most famous for hosting Electric Picnic every year. A festival at the end of the summer where a host of madoutofits go to get gargled and do other activities which for legal reasons I'm not allowed to name. This is all done to the tune of music playing in the fading distance. Ninety per cent of the inhabitants of Electric Picnic spend the entire weekend drinking at their campsite and arguing about whether or not they should go watch Kerri Chandler's set in a forest.

The collective consciousness of Stradbally's self-esteem takes a major beating every Monday after Electric Picnic when thousands of people are feverishly trying to escape from Stradbally. Because on the Monday, for the first time all weekend, the dust settles and they all suddenly realise they are in Stradbally. The local shop in Stradbally has a plaque up with the names of everyone who went to Electric Picnic with the title underneath reading 'the ones who got away'. Nobody's sure if it's a good idea yet. Electric Picnic is not to be confused with Electric Picnics. Electric Picnic is a music festival, Electric Picnics is a Laois-based form of torture where a hungry man from Dublin has to lie on a wet electric blanket.

Many people don't know Laois is the home of motor-racing. It just doesn't seem like that kind of place. Although it turns out the origins of motor-racing began when people tried to race out of Stradbally as quickly as they could. Vroom vroom. Make sure to check out the Steam Rally when you visit Stradbally. It's an annual festival where the locals parade around in their tractors. And for a weekend, they are known as steam enthusiasts instead of farmers. And somehow, people think that this is good!

## *NIGHTLIFE*

The Vintage Inn is the most famous pub in Stradbally, and maybe, the only one. Who knows? I don't bother with the specifics when it comes to my research. The Vintage Inn is a rustic quiet pub with a great pint of Guinness. It didn't get its name because you have to be sixty or over to go there. In fact, it's alleged that this pub only opens during Electric Picnic and for the rest of the year, it's used as the stage set for *Fair City*, although this couldn't possibly be confirmed, because the deadline for this book is coming up and I've really got to keep it moving.

Namaste.

# COUNTY LEITRIM

Sorry, no.

# Carrick-On-Shannon

Carrick-On-Shannon is a small countryside town situated on the banks of the River Shannon. The people of Carrick have been designed by the government to be indecisive by nature. Carrick-On-Shannon has a split personality. Half of the town is in Leitrim and the other half is in Roscommon. Despite all of this, Carrick is still considered the county town of Leitrim. Which really speaks to how much is actually going on in Leitrim.

## Urban myths and legends

Beside the bridge in Carrick lies a Bermuda triangle of takeaway chippers where all dignity and self-respect goes on a walk, never to be found again. At the break of dawn, this is where you'll find a labyrinth of drunk women falling over in high heels along with men from the surrounding countryside areas spilling garlic cheese chips on their Leitrim jerseys while fighting each other.

Everyone in Carrick fondly remembers 'Car Town'. It was a junior disco that they'd all go to as teenagers just to have an excuse to drink in the local GAA pitch before it. This was a favourite place of children who loved getting chased by the Gardaí. It's believed if you entered the pitch on a night with a full moon you'd see them all doing spinnies in the field to get a head rush.

Beside the GAA pitch, for some reason, there's a fire station. A total waste of local resources. There's never been a single fire in Carrick. Due to the low-lying area surrounding the River Shannon, Carrick is basically a non-consensual water park. The town doesn't need a fire station, it would be much better served by a gigantic sponge.

# NIGHTLIFE

There are many bars in Carrick. Some bars where the locals drink pints, and other bars that are on the windows of their homes. Because once you enter the Carrickian realm, no matter how far away you emigrate, you'll eventually end up back here. There is no escape.

Murtagh's is a respectable pub in the heart of Carrick. It's got a friendly atmosphere, great food and they have a special button behind the bar that gets triggered if someone shouts 'Yurtagh Murtagh' loud enough, flinging them directly into the nearby river.

Dunne's is the hub of young adult life in Carrick. It's also the best spot for hen and stag parties in Leitrim. They've never had any, but they've had a divorce party and two wakes. Which is about as close as Leitrim will ever get to metropolitan living.

Last but not least, Cryan's. This is a hotel bar where fully grown emotional men like crying into their pints of Guinness. This isn't because they're sad. It's because their tears dilute the stout so they don't get drunk so easily. They know if they get too drunk, they might actually start sad-crying. And that would be way more embarrassing. Another added benefit from this practice can be found in the hydration the tears provide the drinkers. It's said that this prevents the hangover from kicking in the next day. Although we can't be sure, because no one in this place has ever stopped drinking.

Namaste.

# COUNTY LIMERICK

The media gives Limerick city a hard time, but I don't think they deserve it. Even their statue of King Arthur is holding his sword upside down. The very worst thing people from Limerick will do to you is batter you with the blunt side of a blade.

Yurt.

# Top five things you don't want to miss:

## 1. Shouting 'copper pipe!' on any busy street in Limerick

Limerick is the only place in the world where shouting the words 'copper pipe' on any busy street will make everyone stop whatever they're doing and go look for it so they can steal it off you. This can also be observed when no one is around. If you shout 'copper pipe!' an army of Limerickians will start respawning from the ground to find their beloved treasure and sell it so they can buy more gravy from Chicken Hut.

## 2. Getting stuck talking to a Limerick native about the gravy from Chicken Hut for hours on end

Chicken Hut gravy is to Limerick what burnt spoons are to a Dub. Some say it's the Supermac's of Munster. Don't ever say this to a Limerickian. To them, Chicken Hut is more than a chipper: it's a lifestyle. And they will let you know all about it, even if they have to pin you against the wall and force you to listen to how KFC bought the recipe for their gravy from here, even though they definitely didn't.

## 3. Going to the Crescent shopping centre and asking people if they know Blindboy

This is a fantastic exercise to do if you like practising your social skills on people who definitely don't want to socialise with you.

## 4. Approaching a local and threatening to kidnap Willie O'Dea

You're not going to, obviously. But you definitely could if you wanted to. And sometimes, just knowing that is a comfort in itself.

## 5. Asking someone from Limerick IT to tie your shoelaces

They won't know how and will get so stressed out at this minor inconvenience that they turn it into a three-day party.

**TOXICITY RATING: 7.2**

# Limerick city

Every man woman and child of Limerick city was baptised in the gravy from Chicken Hut. They're dipped in a vat of this sauce by the gatekeeper of Limerick, Tom the accordion player. Tom holds them by the ankles and dunks them in upside down. This develops an Achilles heel in the Limerick locals, so if you kick one of them in the ankle their Chicken Hut loyalty card will dissolve and they'll start going on about Donkey Fords, calling it the best fish and chip shop in the country. Even though it's named after a mule. In the city of Limerick, although blood is thicker than mud, nothing will ever be as thick as the Chicken Hut gravy.

## Urban myths and legends

Limerick has four playable characters, the feen, the beure, the gomie and the gowl.

The feen is the adult male of Limerick, a standard human of urban Munster. He usually drinks too much, he's good at football, he tries to be one of the lads but after a night out usually goes home and plays Wii sports.

Then there's the beure, the female of Limerick. The beure can usually be found on the 304 bus talking really loudly about some feen she's messaging on Snapchat. Similar to the feen, in that when she drinks, she often brings herself to the brink of death. The words feen and beure come from the Irish words 'fion' and 'beor' meaning wine and beer, respectively. So even the genders down here are only an arm's length away from chronic alcoholism.

When a feen and a beure procreate, they'll sometimes give birth to a gomie. The gomie is like the feen, but with higher aggression and lower self-esteem. The gomie will usually be the loudest and most harmless in the social group, a Creme Egg of sorts, hard on the outside with a soft and gooey centre.

The gowl is a close relation to the gomie. A similar character, but slightly more laid back and slightly less intelligent, the gowl is prone to saying the thing they think everyone else is thinking but is too afraid to say out loud. Both gowls and feens are dribblers, but the feen is a good midfielder and the gowl just has saliva issues.

Limerick city has made a huge effort to fight crime in recent years. Due to Limerick winning the three in a row, an amnesty has been set up outside Thomond Park where local youths can hand in their switchblades in exchange for a hurl. It turns out a hurl can be used as a weapon too, but at least it looks like they love sports.

## What else?

Moyross is the most famous tourist destination in Limerick. That's a sentence you'll never hear anyone say. If you're thinking of going to Moyross to ride a horse, that's a great idea, as long as it's only a thought. Moyross is named after a lad called Ross Moy, who changed his name to Moy Ross on Facebook to make the Gardaí think he wasn't selling hash. The Great Wall of Moyross has kept the local residents shivering in the shade for centuries. Many have campaigned to have the wall knocked down, but the government just built them an Iceland instead. The wall has had mixed results within the community of Moyross. It's made them feel like outsiders in a county that wants nothing to do with them, but it's also made them really good at climbing.

College Court is where the students of Limerick go to drop out. If you walk into the centre of this estate and listen closely, you can hear someone shouting 'yurt' every 3.7 seconds. Once the weather reaches above 15 degrees everyone under twenty-five in Limerick comes here to dance and take their tops off. Experts agree that the coronavirus was made in a bathtub in College Court, to create a lockdown just so everyone would come here and take yokes.

'Yurt' is the most frequently used phrase of the Limerickians. It means everything and nothing at the exact same time. The term 'yurt' originated in the caveman era, when a Limerick man from Raheen got his leg stuck in a copper pipe and started screaming for help. Everyone around him misheard him and thought he was saying yurt and as a result he died.

St John's Castle is the stronghold of Limerick culture. This is the geographical mouth that swallows all of Munster's American tourists. It's named after the patron saint of Limerick: John Player Blue. Johnny Blues are locally known as the soother of Southill, because kids love them.

### NIGHTLIFE

Costello's is one of the most famous clubs in Limerick. Flan, the owner, is the unsung hero of Limerick's history. The admission money he collects on the door is used to furnish his flat above the bar: a flat made up entirely of loose fivers.

Costello's in Irish translates to big smoking area, sticky dance floor. The red carpet in Costello's is so old they actually robbed it off Aladdin.

The Icon nightclub used to be home to everyone who

didn't go to Costy's. It got shut down a few years ago due to all the GAA players and countryside students accidentally bumping into each other and spilling bottles of Bulmer's Berry all over each other's bootcut jeans. Some say the Icon was the Supermac's of the nightclub industry. Except instead of getting a burger box you get a box off the bouncer.

Namaste.

# COUNTY LONGFORD

Let's be honest, Longford is weird. The Longford natives didn't experience the same evolution that other humans had. They evolved from bales of hay. This is why they are incapable of experiencing the highs and lows of everyday life. It also explains why they roll into the foetal position and start screaming whenever a horse approaches, in fear that it will nibble at their straw hair.

# Top five things you don't want to miss:

## 1. The bales of hay

This may seem repetitive but let's remember we can't be too picky here. Longford isn't exactly New York. Hay is the national symbol of county hope. The beginning and end of Longfordian consciousness. This is where the locals get their famous phrase from: 'from hay you came, you shall remain, until you are hay again.' Longford people are always hay.

## 2. Not talking about how the cathedral burnt down and seemed to be rebuilt overnight

Who burnt it down? Why didn't anyone ever see it getting rebuilt? It seemed to just appear out of nowhere. The Longfordians like to keep this information to themselves because they are afraid they'll be wrongly outed as closeted Scientologists and hung from a crucifix in the town square.

## 3. Watching the locals wait until it's time to move to Dublin

Longford, like most of the Midlands, is a launchpad of mass emigration. A geographical waiting room. The locals here are all in the grips of a blackout until the day they wake up, outside some meat-packing factory in Dublin, wondering how long until someone comes to kill them.

## 4. Frozen pizza

Most frozen pizza in the country is made in Longford. The locals love it so much that they usually eat it straight from the packet. In Longford, ovens are useless. They just get in the way of the truth.

## 5. Getting a Longford native to talk about Blazers so you can steal their wallet

Longfordians are blinded by Midlands-based nostalgia. Get one of them to start talking about the two-euro drinks they used to buy in Blazers if you want to launch them into a tirade about how Longford hasn't been the same since they shut down. When someone from Longford gets nostalgic they go numb, which is one of their only three states; the other two are jealousy and outrage. The numbness will stop them feeling you robbing a wallet out of their pocket.

**TOXICITY RATING: 9.3**

# Longford town

Longford town is the county town of Longford. Historically, Longford was a garrison town for the British military. But the Brits soon fled Longford, because the boredom nearly killed them. Some argue the state of Longford is the reason Ireland gained independence from the grip of colonial rule in 1922.

Longford is basically at the centre of Ireland, which means Longfordians are as far away from the sea as is humanly possible. This is for the best, because if the locals of Longford town were let loose on the beach, they wouldn't know what to do with themselves.

Longford is still a bustling town because all the aspiring locals stay here in the hopes that they'll magically be granted a pharmaceutical job in Abbott. Which they inevitably leave after a couple of weeks when they realise it doesn't actually give them access to the same back pain medication they've been stealing from their granny's cabinet.

## What you'll find here

Razorblade Alley is the focal point of the Longfordian experience. This is a famous lane where Longford people shave off their beards for the first time. At this point in their life, their beards are unkempt and overgrown. They usually go to the alley for their long-overdue shave, a couple of weeks after their first holy communion. These people are known as the Longford child-men. They develop neckbeards in their mother's womb. This is a protective measure that the Longfordians have evolved to hide their facial tattoos.

When visiting Longford, why not pop into the site that turned Longford into the town it is today? Longford shopping centre. This shopping centre keeps the Longfordians trapped in a never-ending shopping spree. This consumerist cult was invented by Tesco. Tesco is the dictator of taste and opinion in Longford, which is why everyone in Longford wears plastic Tesco shopping bags instead of real clothes. The shopping centre features a concentration of people who say things like 'meet me at the shopping centre' and then spend the rest of the day wandering around Longford shopping centre, stealing.

Luigi's takeaway in the town is the main site of edible worship. Despite its name, not a single Italian has ever been inside Luigi's. But once the garlic cheese chips find their way into your mouth, you might set up a tent inside the shop and live there for the rest of your life. The legend goes that the chips in Luigi's are famously chunky due to the staff not being bothered cutting the chips, but this isn't true; they actually cut the chips with a spoon.

## NIGHTLIFE

Nope.

Namaste.

# COUNTY LOUTH

Louth is known as the wee county, because it's the smallest county in Ireland and also because everyone here loves getting pissed on. While it may be the tiniest county in the country, it has the highest concentration of people capable of shattering glass with nothing but their loud voices. This is something the locals typically do when drunk on public transport – which, in Louth, is actually more common than being sober on public transport. They say a person from Louth even has loud thoughts; loud, Louth thoughts. Some would say Louth is in the North by technicality. It's not in the IRA, but they've definitely been to some of the same house parties together.

## Top five things you don't want to miss:

**1. Trying get someone from Dundalk to say the words 'Mars bar'**
They can't do it. Unfortunately, Dundalkians don't know how to speak properly due to all those years of inhaling the toxic fumes from Sellafield.

**2. Asking someone from Drogheda if they're from Dundalk**
If you would like to scare yourself to tears.

**3. Taking a trip to the Cooley Mountains**
A really quick trip. Do this after number 2 on the list. But only if you are afraid of Drogheda and want to get as far away as possible.

**4. Going to Carlingford**
Peel back the layers of the Instagram aesthetic and see that Carlingford is just a tourist trap full of sad old men pubs with a deafening flurry of fake Northern accents.

**5. Asking one of the locals about the mystery of Funtasia**
Who still goes there? How is it still open? And why is it that everyone in Bettystown seems to have a friend who works there?

## TOXICITY RATING: 9.4

# Dundalk

Dundalkians have their own language. It's a bit like English, just with three words at the end of each sentence that add nothing to its overall structure, such as 'so there is', 'so I am', 'so we are'. People from Dundalk sound like they have invisible Curly Wurlys in their mouth. Outsiders can never understand what they're saying, so we must watch for their facial expressions.

## Local cuisine

The Roma is an ancient food coliseum in the town. This fortress of fish and chips has been a constant in the lives of Dundalkians who fear change. The Roma has been the first meeting place of all happy couples in Dundalk, because Dundalkians think battered sausages are romantic.

## Urban myths and legends

Dundalk is the home of the ham child, the offspring of a Drogheda local who procreated with a farmhouse pig, creating this poultry-based human life-form. These ham children flock to their local temple, Sing Li. The entrepreuners behind the van realised if they were serving food to the ham children of Dundalk, they'd need to be able to escape quickly. When Dundalkians engage in a confrontation, at a certain point they stop shouting and engage with physical contact, the process when words turn to violence is called Dun-dalking.

Muirhevnamor is known as the Florida of Louth, because it's where Republicans come to retire. Some say Muirhevnamor is just an extension of Belfast, but I don't think it deserves the title. If you were to throw a rock in the park here, there's only a 40 per cent chance it would hit a member of the Wolfetones in the head.

The bogeyman of Muirhevnamor has been haunting the estate since time began. It's believed that if you walk through Muirhevnamor at night and utter the words 'Soonie John what's goin an', Soonie himself will float into the atmosphere and hassle you until you buy him a bag of chips from Sorrento's with extra vinegar.

The minimum wage in Dundalk is seven euro an hour. Because seven euro used to be enough to buy six cans of Harp. Drinking six cans of Harp an hour is enough to make you almost forget that you live in Drogheda's shadow. In more recent times, the price of Harp shot up dramatically, which forced Dundalkians to buy their cans in Newry just because it was slightly cheaper.

The Dundalkians have been recovering from a spiritual earthquake in 2013 when the old shopping centre got knocked down and was converted into a Tesco. The neoliberal economy of Dundalkia was indifferent to the plight of its people, instead pandering to an imagined future of never-ending shopping lists and loose trolleys. It's reported Dundalkians hate Tesco almost as much as they hate Drogheda. But nowhere near as much as they hate themselves for not stopping the demolition when they had the chance.

## NIGHTLIFE

The Spirit Store is a magical place where hipsters summon their dead relatives. Invoking the spirits is always a bad idea as they usually make fun of the living hipster for their art-studenty ways, then the lights come on and the hipsters go home questioning whether they should've pursued a career in finance instead.

Namaste.

# Drogheda

According to Droghedians, Drogheda is split into two sides, the far side and the far side. No one knows which side the far side is truly on, because Drogheda natives are too stubborn to admit they're wrong. The illusion of the far side, or 'the fah side' as it's locally known, was created because Droghedians needed an enemy, so they had to argue amongst themselves, because Dundalkians were too scared of them. Even though Dundalk is just Drogheda with narcissistic personality disorder. People in Drogheda can't pronounce their R's. This is because the River Boyne found its way into their tap water and gave them a speech impediment. In Drogheda the R's become aw's, because they think everything is so cute.

## What you'll find here

Scotch Hall is a social hub where businesses go to shut down. Scotch Hall is a weapon of biological warfare, this shopping centre has an energy field that makes Droghedian children do laps around it while they're meant to be in school. This spell gets broken once they are old enough to drink in the local parks, which is usually around the age of 10.

Funtasia Water Park landed in Drogheda as a social experiment to frighten the locals, who have been scared of swimming pools ever since the water shortages of 2017. The government thought it would be funny to put a water park in Drogheda because no one in Drogheda ever asked for it. If you type the question 'What's the opposite of Funtasia?' into Google, a picture of Drogheda will come up.

Half of this town are just clueless people from Dublin that think everywhere outside the capital is a cattle market. They got lured here thinking that Drogheda would offer them a peaceful life in the countryside. Whenever Drogheda natives leave the town, all they seem to be able to talk about is how they have cousins in Dublin. Because people from Drogheda think Navan is in Dublin.

There's a museum in Drogheda. No one has ever been inside it, because Droghedians live eternally in the moment and have absolutely no regard for history or culture. Some of my researchers snuck inside and apparently it's an underground stone passageway that stretches for thousands of miles with an empty altar at the end of it that has the words 'FUCK DUNDALK' spray-painted on it.

St Peter's Church used to be a place of worship but now it's a courtyard for teenagers to practise doing wheelies. The main attraction of St Peter's Church is the preserved head of St Oliver, who lives inside the chapel. Because someone, somewhere, thought that would be a good idea. Many critics believe this head was stolen from the set of *The Mummy Returns*, while others say the facial expression looks like a man who just lost his house keys on a really slow rollercoaster in Funtasia.

## NIGHTLIFE

Fusion and Earth are the two main nightclubs in Drogheda. Everyone who goes to Earth looks the exact same, and they all have the same thoughts, usually, *I'm hungry*, or *I'm tired*, or *yup the town*. Fusion is where the alternative crowd go. The hipsters in Drogheda are a lot more dangerous than the hipsters in other parts of the world because their accent is so unique. If you ask them to repeat themselves they'll go quiet, stick on Nirvana in their noise-cancelling headphones and refuse to talk, because you just confirmed their belief that nobody gets them and they are deeply misunderstood.

Namaste.

# Ardee

Ardee is a market town in the smallest county in Ireland. Wedged between Dundalk and Drogheda, Ardee often had to act as a translator to the outside world, deciphering the Morse code of the Dundalkian dialect. Ardee is situated on a rolling green landscape, not because of its fields or hills, simply because it's the only place the Drogheda boys can smoke a joint without getting pulled over by the Gardaí. Because there are no Gardaí in Ardee. There are just disgruntled Ardee locals who go around on bikes waiting to perform a citizen's arrest on any lawbreakers caught in the act. These are known as the Gardee.

The Ardee folk are generally a friendly breed. Constantly using the word 'hey' as an exclamation point at the end of a sentence. This can at first seem confusing to visitors, as it feels like you have to say 'hey' back to them, but the visitors get used to it once they walk away and refuse to travel to Ardee again because it's far too confusing.

## Urban myths and legends

It's believed Ardee in Irish translates to 'massive family of cousins'. This strong blood-relation line in Ardee is felt in the spirit of the community. Everyone knows each other and there's a wonderful sense of unity amongst the locals. Even if they do experience unnatural urges from time to time. In Ardee, the local catchphrase is 'keep it in the family' and one thing you can never say about Ardeeians is that they don't stick to their principles.

In medieval times, Ardee was situated at the very northern border of the Pale, an area occupied by the British government. As a result Ardee seems to think it needs two castles. There's Ardee Castle and Hatch's Castle. Ardee Castle is situated in the centre of the town. It's believed its sole purpose was to get to the top and overlook Kells, so they could judge them for not having a castle and living in the past. Hatch's Castle is more like a bed and breakfast with an owner so friendly that you almost forget that the windows were used to shoot arrows at people a few hundred years ago.

There are too many statues in Ardee, but perhaps the most famous one was originally believed to depict Cúchulainn and Ferdia, two characters of Irish mythology. This claim turns out to be false, as people from Ardee think Irish mythology is weird. The statue is actually of two lads who got in a fight after being kicked out of Lúna for sharing a garlic cheese chips on the dancefloor.

# Carlingford

Carlingford is a coastal town in Louth. It was invaded by the Vikings and was originally called Kerlingfjǫrðr, but the locals soon changed it back to Carlingford because no one had time to learn the original spelling. Remnants of Carlingford's Viking heritage can still be sensed amongst the locals, who can't stop shouting and running around with swords on boats. The name Kerlingfjǫrðr translates to sea-inlet of the hag, which the Carlingford natives didn't like so much. They hate when people talk about their mother like that.

## What you'll find here

The crown jewel of Carlingford is the Carlingford Adventure Centre. It's a famous hotspot for schoolchildren all over the country, who would go on a school trip here when the school budget didn't stretch to Funderland. Usually only one class in any school gets to go to Carlingford, the rest of them have the pleasure of staying away. As a result, Carlingford Adventure Centre has remained a social construct in the minds of the children who never went there. This construct was usually followed by a chortle and a grunt that sounded like 'ha ha, Carlingford'. The kids who did have the opportunity to visit the adventure centre loved it, because it's easy to convince children that climbing a giant rock wall and shooting people with lasers in a forest constitutes 'an adventure'. When will these kids ever learn, there's really no greater adventure than walking up to strangers at the bus stop and pretending to be a messenger from the future who needs their bank details in order to perpetuate the human race.

Another fascinating element of life in Carlingford can be found up in the Cooley Mountains. It's believed that leprechaun bones were found on the Cooley Mountains back in 1989. This led to an annual leprechaun hunt that has been held here ever since. Unfortunately, no one ever found a leprechaun, perhaps because they're too hard to catch, or perhaps because the leprechaun bones were actually the bones of a really small man who froze to death. Carlingford then decided to capitalise on this man's death and immortalise his legacy by pretending he was a leprechaun. When no one is around and the leprechaun tour has finished for the evening, the leprechauns all come out of their caverns and watch videos on YouTube of American tourists. Leprechauns love them. The American tourists always believed in them when no one else would. This nightly event leads to endless hours of streaming content, because the Wi-Fi on the mountain is excellent.

## NIGHTLIFE

The nightlife in Carlingford is awash with hens and stags. No one knows how these animals escaped the farm, but there aren't enough tranquillising darts to stop all of them falling around and destroying the town every weekend. This has become a solemnly accepted fact of the locals who try to stay away from the town after 10 p.m. as a result.

PJ's oyster bar is where you can find the remains of the leprechaun bones. The pub was named after the late great PJ O Hare, who was the man that encountered the remains on the Cooley Mountains all those years back. As a result of this and their delicious sea food, this has become a bustling hub of tourist activity. This is the only pub where you can enjoy a creamy Guinness beside a gaggle of drunk hens from Newcastle asking if you know where to find any real-life skeletons of really small men.

Namaste.

## Termonfeckin

Everybody told me not to do it. They said Ireland isn't ready to hear the truth.

Today I'd like to address the question of Termonfeckin. For centuries, Termonfeckin has been the butt of the joke. Many have argued the only reason people go to Termonfeckin is to go to the beach, but the beach is actually in Clogherhead, an area completely separate to Termonfeckin. There's an adult education centre in Termonfeckin called An Grianán. This centre was originally set up by the Irish Countrywomen Association. Although it's original ethos was seeped in a pro-women liberation of feminist thought, they have since regressed, with most people now going there to learn how to knit. An Grianán has excellent reviews online. The Termonfeckians can't help but notice they've never seen anyone leave or enter the building. The word 'grianán' in Irish means 'sunny place'; which is ironic, as it's alleged that the inside of this centre is actually a really dark cave.

## Urban myths and legends

There's a coffee shop in Termonfeckin called The Forge. It's loved by locals and visitors alike, despite its dark secret. This coffee shop in Termonfeckin doesn't have any coffee in it, so if you ask for a flat white they'll just give you a cup of boiling water and milk. Termonfeckians can't tell the difference. And even if they could, it wouldn't matter. Everyone from Termonfeckin drinks tea. It would be far too dangerous to caffeinate the people of Termonfeckin. They'd develop an overblown ego and start acting like they're from Dundalk.

Termonfeckin is home to many of the elite of Dublin who valued living in a quaint village that has nothing in it. This village is often referred to as D.O.D. (the Donnybrook of Drogheda). Partly due to the huge villas and wide open spaces, and partly due to the fact that if you trespass on someone's estate, they have the right to shoot you with an assault weapon.

Termonfeckin boasts one of the busiest petrol stations in the country. From dusk til dawn it's loaded to the brim with people desperately buying as much petrol as possible so they can leave Termonfeckin forever.

It's commonly known that if you walk through Termonfeckin and say 'Is this it?' The girl who played Luna Lovegood in Harry Potter will appear under the bridge and ferociously start talking about herself for 25 minutes. Her self-involved diatribe is meant to distract you from realising the uneventful reality of life in Termonfeckin itself. Amidst her ranting and raving, the only part you'll decipher is something along the lines of how she doesn't want people to get confused, she may have played a wizard on the silver screen but in real life she always carries her angel cards in her back pocket and believes in big witch energy.

## *NIGHTLIFE*

The heart of Termonfeckin can be found in an area simply known as 'the lane'. The lane is not to be confused with any other lanes surrounding it. It's not to be confused, because there are no other lanes in Termonfeckin. Despite all protests from the elders of Termonfeckin, who don't need to drink in the lane because they are old enough to go to Flynn's, the lane has become a humble space of social learning for the youth of this quiet village. This is where all young Termonfeckian youths learn how to be unattractive to the opposite sex and how not to drink.

Namaste.

# COUNTY MAYO

The Mayo natives are a simple, kind folk. Real bacon-and-cabbage people. The Mayo puritans have been colonised by holiday-home buyers, usually people from South Dublin or Greystones who invade Westport and contaminate the area with their twenty-first-century ideas. People from Mayo believe these posh intruders are poisoning the Mayo genome. Mayoians are taking part in a human race of condiment culture. They wish to exterminate all privileged outsiders who consume honey mustard and smashed avocado. Mayo are total white supremacists, in the sense that all Mayo can tolerate is Mayo.

# Top five things you don't want to miss:

### 1. Getting arrested by a Garda from Mayo
In Mayo it has been shown that there are on average 120 guards per 100 people. Not only does this mean that everyone in Mayo is a guard, it also means that 20 per cent of guards are not people, they are a different species entirely. Superintendents.

### 2. Asking about the real Mayo curse
But try to insist that it's got nothing to do with football and it's actually to do with people who eat mayo straight out of the jar and then realise that nobody loves them.

### 3. The Mayo flamethrow
This consists of a man from Ballyhaunis well into his thirties who farts into a lit flame from a Zippo lighter that you're holding. He doesn't ask for your permission. The Ballyhaunis man is an agile creature and can assume the position while you're trying to light a smoke. His friends have all left Ballyhaunis for Australia, while he's still trapped in a never-ending cycle of passing gas and watching life go by, but he's still getting the last laugh.

### 4. Watching the locals that forget to emigrate sink directly into a bog
To the uninitiated this might seem like a cruel process, but in Mayo, it's a necessary step to get rid of people who wouldn't ever have made it as guards anyway.

### 5. Achill Island
Achill Island is a great place to go for people who can't handle real life and need to escape to somewhere where they will find it more difficult to fuck everything up. Visit Achill Island if you'd like to see where all the disinherited sons and daughters of D4 families live.

# Kiltimagh

Kiltimagh is a small country town in Mayo. Despite its obscure existence, many famous people hail from here, including Louis Walsh and a bunch of other people who stare at you while you're singing. Kiltimagh is known to be a picturesque village of nineteenth-century architecture. Which is the era Kiltimagh is stuck in, or more specifically, the Famine. Kiltimagh is the birthplace of Irish-speaking poet Raifteirí. He was blind, obviously. If he could see he would have run for the hills, Slieve Carn, to be exact. It's only a quarter of a kilometre outside the town, and no one in Kiltimagh ever dares travel any further than that, because cars don't exist there yet. Kiltimagh is equidistant from Sligo, Galway, Westport and Achill. This has led to a geographical game of hot potato with tourists passing through the lonely lanes of Kiltimagh, only to make a pit stop to laugh.

## Urban myths and legends

'Kiltimagh used to be a busy centre of industry' is not a sentence anyone has ever said before. But they used to have a train station. They got rid of it in the 1960s when they realised no one ever needed to use it, eventually turning the train station into something far more useful: a museum. The museum of Kiltimagh is an excellent resource for the community as it allows them to have one foot in the past, and the other in the past.

It's believed the word 'culchie' traces its origins in Kiltimagh. Not because the word is a derivative of the town itself, it's because the children born here drive tractors out of the womb and everyone wears wellies while they're sleeping so they're ready to roll out of bed and scrape turf out of the bog at 5 a.m. On the rare occasion that the locals venture out of Kiltimagh, whenever someone asks them where they're from, they keep calling Kiltimagh 'never mind'.

When visiting Kiltimagh, why not go for a stroll on one of the town's countryside walks. These are known as the Kiltimagh loops. The loop of Kiltimagh is a memory lapse in which you're walking in a field and Louis Walsh keeps popping out of the bush and forgetting he doesn't live here anymore. The truth is, the real Louis Walsh never left Kiltimagh, because Kiltimagh wouldn't allow it. So BBC created a Louis Walsh lookalike to become a celebrity judge on talent shows and to manage successful boybands while the real Louis Walsh rode around the town half naked on a horse.

## NIGHTLIFE

Teach O'Hora's is an idyllic Irish pub steeped in tradition, or as they call it *'ceol agus craic'*, which usually just means there's a drunk old man playing a bodhrán in the corner while staring into the endless void of easy-listening countryside-living. Teach O'Hora's got it's name from a compromise on the original name which allegedly was 'Teach A Horse How to Lay Down in a Bar'. A name, which, much like Kiltimagh itself, turned out to be a pointless endeavour. Animals wouldn't come near this place. Horses hate Irish music.

Namaste

# Ballyhaunis

Ballyhaunis is a rustic settlement off the coast of Mayo. Ballyhaunis has a self-regulating government ever since the people cordoned themselves off from the rest of Ireland after that Denny's ad due to shame. Ballyhaunis is often known as the town that time forgot. I don't think that's a fair statement. Ballyhaunis isn't a town, it's a village. Time is not a pressing matter in Ballyhaunis. If you were to ask someone in Ballyhaunis what time it is they'll simply say 'No, thank you.'

Upon entering Ballyhaunis, you may notice unpleasant smell wafting through the air. Alternatively, you may not have nostrils, which is the only way you'd drive through Ballyhaunis without passing a comment such as 'for fuck sake, who died?'

## Urban myths and legends

Despite all that can be said about Ballyhaunis, according to the 2016 Census it's the most multicultural village in Ireland, claiming that over half of the local residents are of non-Irish ethnicity. Although Ballyhaunis has successfully embraced modernity, further investigation shows that visitors from different countries must really love boredom. Every time you hear the words 'Ballyhaunis' and 'cosmopolitan living' in the same sentence, you can't help but smile and wonder of all the places a human being can choose to live, why would it ever be a village in Mayo?

With all the ringforts, souterrains and other megalithic sites around the village, Ballyhaunis is an archaeologist's wet dream. But because archaeologist's can't cum, it just makes them groan with pleasure like they've been rudely awoken from a really sexy nightmare.

## NIGHTLIFE

The Midas nightclub used to be the main nightclub in Ballyhaunis. Like all nightclubs in the west of Ireland, The Midas wasn't really a nightclub. It was a jiving hall where old people from Mayo could become semi-physically intimate while drunkenly whispering Christy Moore lyrics in each others' ears. The children of Ballyhaunis grew up going to Monsoon. It was the underage disco in the village and a temple of vomit and public urination. This is where the Ballyhaunis youth congregated with the youths of Ballinasloe, who arrived down on a bus every weekend. A strange metaphysical phenomena occurs once these teens become too old to attend the underage disco. Once the clock strikes midnight on their eighteenth birthday they instantly turn fifty-six to blend in with the rest of Ballyhaunis.

Namaste.

## Castlebar

Castlebar is the county town of Mayo. This town is immersed in history, with strong links to the 1798 rebellion. It used to be a garrison for British soldiers before Ireland gained independence as a sovereign state, but no one really cares. Castlebar got its name as a tribute to the King of Mayo's estate, King Enda Kenny. His castle is made entirely out of chocolate bars with a printed photo of him sticking his thumb up on them. King Enda also built a state-of-the-art swimming complex in Castlebar, to which he appointed himself ruler. The mystical properties of the pool water made it so that if you tried swimming in it and you weren't a Fine Gael back-bencher, you'd sink like a stone. Enda Kenny had scientists working on this magical pool for years. It was specifically designed so that if Enda ever wanted to go for a swim, gravity would become non-essential and it would feel like he was an astronaut. Unfortunately, once the pool saw

Enda Kenny nursing the devastating combo of a blotchy farmer's tan with a tight pair of red speedos, all the water ran out of the pool due to fear.

## What you'll find here

The main park of Castlebar is known as The Mall. It used to be a cricket pitch for British settler Lord Lucan and his family. The Mall used to also be a place for public hangings, but thankfully this cruel ritual has long since left the town of Castlebar. It's been about four weeks.

Lough Lannagh is where the youth of Castlebar and the surrounding areas who don't have lakes go to drink themselves into oblivion.

The Museum of Countryside Life is a place where tourists who accidentally go to Castlebar often find themselves. Having said that, it's not very popular amongst the Irish-American community. Simply because there's no such thing as the Irish-American community. It's just the American community who claim they're Irish. To them, this museum goes down like a house on fire. It's where visitors can uncover what it's like to be a farmer. It turns out, it feels like being underpaid and drunk.

### NIGHTLIFE

The emos and skaters of Castlebar actually exist. They are the outliers and you can spot them easily because they'll be the ones that never have a hurl in their hand. They generally congregate underneath the bridge of Castletown, listening to My Chemical Romance while nursing a semi-serious chemical romance of their own. They can be found posting a blurry picture on their Snapchat story saying something like *'Whoz comin bridge xx'*.

Namaste.

## Cong

Cong is a tiny village in Mayo. It's the least exotic exotic-sounding place on earth. Everyone in Cong still brags about how it's home to the Hollywood elite, just because *A Quiet Man* was filmed here in 1952.

Many American tourists who think they're Irish make their way to Cong to discover themselves, but they just discover that Cong has nothing in it. The locals of Cong embrace the Americans and adore them as heroes, begging them to bring them back to America so they can escape the treacheries of this sleepy territory.

## Urban myths and legends

The entire economy of Cong rests on the five-star shoulders of a luxury hotel they call Ashford Castle. They decided to keep the name 'Ashford Castle' instead of Ashford hotel, because Ashford hotel sounds like the name of a place that would fit right into a Netflix murder documentary. So, Ashford Castle, is no longer a castle.

It's believed the village of Cong has been cryogenically frozen since 1952, out of respect for *The Quiet Man,* the most forward-thinking piece of media that ever came out of Mayo. Also, the only piece of media that ever came out of Mayo. The famous cottage where many scenes of the film took place has been preserved in its original state for tourists to trip over themselves and make a mess.

## What you'll find here

Walking through the cobbled streets of Cong wakes all the locals up, who can often sleep for days at a time. Because in Cong, that's all there is to do. The very fact that there is a human lifeform walking through Cong is an event in itself.

Make sure when visiting Cong to take a peaceful stroll down through Cong Abbey, literally and figuratively as far away from Abbey Street as you could ever get. This walkway is really where you see the 1950s come to life. Everyone here wears a farmer's cap and waves at you, and if you squint your eyes, you might see someone fondling a sheep.

*NIGHTLIFE*

No.
Namaste.

# Belmullet

Belmullet is a Gaeltacht town, which means the older people in the area can speak Irish when they're sober enough to use their mouth, while the younger people have names like 'Fionn' or 'Ruairi'. They chain-smoke cheap cigarettes outside the local entertainment centre (the shop) and wear so much hair gel that you can smell it. There's a magical force field in Belmullet that protects the little town from the havoc of gentrification, forbidding motorways, supermarkets, shopping centres or chain stores from entering the vicinity, allowing Belmullet to continue to flourish as the remote, random place that it is. Belmullet is essentially a science experiment conducted by Charlie Haughey back in the '80s to see what would happen if you put a small village in a time capsule shielded from the treachery and technology of the outside world. As a result, Belmullet recently discovered the use of microwaves, before which they were cooking eggs in their hands by trying to get as close to the sun as possible.

## Urban myths and legends

Belmullet is a well-known stop-off point for tourists travelling across the Wild Atlantic Way. While most think the Wild Atlantic Way is a 2,500-km tourism trail that journeys through the coast of Ireland, when these adventurers make their way to Belmullet they realise the Wild Atlantic Way is just an old shoeless man pulling the tail off a feral pig while he asks you for money to go to the bookie's so he can win his family back.

When visiting Belmullet make sure to bring a surfboard, as water sports are very popular down here. Not with the locals obviously, but make sure to come down here in a Dryrobe and a wetsuit if you'd like to be the talk of the town for a week, they'll be convinced you're wearing alien technology and will try to fish you out of the water to get you to explain to them what forex trading is all about.

Everyone in Belmullet has a mullet, obviously. It's one of the only requirements for the citizens who live there. It's situated on the bottom of the mullet peninsula in the barony of Erris. Erris was considering getting rid of Belmullet completely, chopping the Belmullet to get a Beldryfade, a number one on the back and sides, but when Belmullet caught wind of this, the locals stood together in solidarity and grew their mullets even longer, started using MSN messenger again and carried hair straighteners in their pockets for protection.

Namaste.

# COUNTY MEATH

Meath is a majestical place of confusion. Meath is segregated into North and South Meath. South Meath thinks they're Dublin's fake nail extension. North Meath is almost a different breed entirely. The young people all have the mental age of a sharp 65-year-old. They say the further north you go in Meath the less you can understand the accent. At the most northerly point of Meath, the locals are reduced to shouts and grunts, so just smile and hope they don't bash in your skull with a rock.

# Top five things you don't want to miss:

### 1. Ratoath living in Dunshaughlin's shadow

Ratoath and Dunshaughlin have been in constant battle with each other. This gets conditioned into the children who are taught to hate each other at an early age, usually when playing football against each other in the NDSL. They say when Dunshaughlin Youths come head to head with the Ratoath Harps, it creates a dent in the Dunshaughlin–Ratoath peace treaty and brings any progression to a screeching halt. Dunshaughlin is obviously a better place than Ratoath and always has been. But this fact has been confirmed yet again by the swarms of Ratoath natives who have to swallow their pride and flock to Dunshaughlin to do their shopping. Because Dunshaughlin has both an Aldi and a Lidl.

### 2. Watching criminals from Dublin play hide-and-seek from the Gardaí

Meath is a great holiday destination for people who are on the run from law enforcement. This game of hide-and-seek takes ages because once they enter the realm of Meath no one knows where they disappeared to because the Gardaí think that crime doesn't happen here. There might only be like two Garda stations in Meath, and one of them is in Ashbourne, which doesn't count because Ashbourne is basically Dublin.

### 3. Observing the Louth–Meath–Dublin paradox

People from Louth are fake Meath, people from Meath are fake Dublin, people from Dublin are fake Canada Goose enthusiasts. To the people of Meath, Louth is a distant concept. Louth is the attention-seeking little brother of Meath, but they don't know that whenever they try to copy Meath, Meath will just hate them more, but it's not because Meath hates Louth. Meath hates itself. As for Dublin, Dublin is just too out of its head to realise they're all part of the same family.

## 4. Observing the overblown egos of people from Trim

The only thing people in Trim ever say is 'Up Trim, fuck Navan.' They are so obsessed with fucking Navan maybe they should get a room and just get it over with. Ancient reports suggest that Navan and Trim had a baby out of wedlock, which is how Kells was born. No wonder they hate each other. Their child is a boring loser with nothing going on other than country music. Kells have tried to get themselves on the map by feuding with Navan. But this is a bit like Steve Irwin's kid trying to be the next Steve Irwin even though he's probably terrified of crocodiles.

## 5. Marvelling at the randomness of the Bus Éireann buses

Buses in Meath are a rare phenomenon. The buses don't have timetables here, they have emotions. Whether or not a bus comes depends entirely on the whims of the bus itself. If a bus is feeling happy, it'll eventually arrive, always with at least two of the same buses. This is because the bus likes to arrive with another bus that's feeling depressed and drives straight by the bus stop because it doesn't want to be around people.

## TOXICITY SCORE: 6.3

## Navan

Navan is the New York of Meath. Navan is spelt the same way back to front. To lessen the confusion already experienced by the Navan locals, a population made up entirely of dyslexics. Navan is locally known as 'Naaaaavan', because adding more vowels to the start of the word gives them more time to remember what they were talking about. No one knows what came first, Cavan or Navan, no one except me. It was Cavan, Cavan tried to call Navan 'Car-van' and Navan said 'Nah, van', and so it has been ever since.

## Urban myths and legends

The Bull statue in the centre of the town has mystical powers. Its aura forces drunk Navan natives to jump on its back after a night out. It's safe to ride the bull at night because he's asleep. But no one has ever rode the bull during the day, in case he decides to take off and start running.

Everyone knows Hector, Dylan Moran and Tommy Tiernan are from Navan, but no one ever sees them in the same room together, because they're the same person. They just split the week into shifts so no one gets too tired of being famous and talented. Pierce Brosnan is from Navan too and has made it his life's mission to try and hide it, even going as far as becoming James Bond, who, as everyone knows, is the polar opposite of Navan.

The Navan shopping centre is a black hole that keeps the Navan natives in a perpetual cycle of not knowing what shops to go into, before walking into Tesco and then going home. This shopping centre used to have a maze in it, but ironically enough, they got rid of it, because it was really hard to find.

The locals of Navan famously replaced Catholicism with their new religion: Navanism, or the sacred worship of the NX bus. This was a godsend to the Navan locals because it went straight from Navan to the city centre without any stops along the way, meaning Navanites wouldn't have to mix with anyone that's not from Navan.

The Ramparts is a fragile ecosystem, home of the morning joggers and enthusiastic naggin drinkers, along with a sprinkling of full-time alcoholics. The naggin drinkers judge both the joggers and the alcoholics, not knowing in ten years time, they'll end up becoming one or the other. In other words, the Ramparts is the only place in Navan where you'll find people trying to improve their lives right next to people who are actively trying to destroy theirs. The Ramparts is all flatland but no one noticed how pointless the name was, because no one in Navan knows what the word 'ramparts' means.

The question of Johnstown has been puzzling Johnstinians for centuries, but everyone else is pretty clear on the matter, despite what the Johnstown natives say, Johnstown is in Navan, it's not a separate country just because they have their own SuperValu and all the houses look the same.

## NIGHTLIFE

Despite its name the Solar nightclub in the basement of the Newgrange Hotel closed its doors a few years ago due to a lack of lighting and everyone accidentally spilling drink on each other. The Navan locals had to emigrate to somewhere else, and all that was left was the only other nightclub in Navan. The Palace nightclub became the meeting spot for the young adults of Navan who wanted to be on Love Island. But the furthest they ever got to was Nobber's Got Talent. The bouncers in the Palace were always known for being friendly, some say they put the 'PAL' in Palace. Most people endured the Palace just to go to the Valley after it. Where they'd slump outside drooling into a garlic cheese chips while howling at the moon and drunkenly cursing god for the futility of existence.

Namaste.

# Dunboyne

Dunboyne is a quaint town in the south of Meath. This area has seen rapid growth in the last twenty years. Many have succumbed to Dunboyne's irresistibly sleepy charm. The locals have become accustomed to the slow pace of life here. Studies show 30 per cent of them have fallen asleep standing up at least twice within the last thirty days.

## Urban myths and legends

SuperValu is the control centre of Dunboyne. A pantheon of productivity. A hive of Dunboynian industry during the day. A vacuous wormhole that leads you to Ashbourne at night time. In SuperValu, you never know who you'll bump into. Sometimes you might bump into someone who has been dead for 20 years. Because Dunboyne is a ghost town.

Dunboyne is that small patch of oblivion nestled between Meath and Dublin. It can only be described as a geographical crossover episode on a Netflix docuseries that never finished getting made. This town is a microcosm of life itself. It's one of the few places in the country where you can smell weed, burnt-out cars, fairtrade coffee and cow shit, all within a 100-metre radius of each other. Like in many other regions in South Meath, Dunboyners either want to be from Dublin or from the countryside. There is a small subsection of Dunboyne purists who believe Dunboyne is better than everywhere else. Although they're not really sure, because if Dunboyne isn't Dublin or the countryside, it's just a friendly SuperValu with a mild accent.

## NIGHTLIFE

The pubs in Dunboyne are definitely some of the best pubs in Dunboyne. Brady's is famous for pulling one of the best pints of Guinness. It's a favourite meeting place of respectable Sunday afternoon drinkers, who usually bring their kids in after Mass to eat packets of Tayto and TK Red Lemonade while they drink. If you didn't grow up spending your childhood in Brady's on a Sunday, you weren't happy. Brady's is also a fan favourite of teachers and Gardaí. So if you happen to be breaking the law, or go to the local school, stay out!

Slevin's pub caters to a slightly younger crowd, mainly because, unlike Brady's, there's a TV in here and the lunch menu serves burritos. The TV was an insightful move on their part, because if there's one thing millennials hate more than anything else while socialising with other people, it's socialising with other people.

O'Dwyers is another pub in the town. This is a classy bar, home to the sophisticated Dunboynians who enjoy drinking cocktails and pretending they're James Bond. The food in here is next to none. Sometimes the local hero of Dunboyne can be found in here, his name is Jimmy and he owns the pub. Jimmy always goes above and beyond to make sure all of his patrons feel welcome. Allegedly when the clock strikes twelve every night in this bar, everyone stands up for the national anthem while Jimmy does a cartwheel and tells everyone he loves them.

Namaste.

# Duleek

Duleek is a small village on the border of Meath. Duleek is often known as 'Da Leak' due to the fact that plumbers don't exist here. If you lived in Duleek and you asked someone to come to your house to fix your kitchen sink, they'd never find you. The government wiped Duleek off the Google Maps of handymen.

The village exists in a state of rural frustration. This is mainly down to the fact that it is seven miles away from the beach. Which is just far away enough to justify never needing to go there.

## Urban myths and legends

Duleek is home to the first stone church in Ireland. This village has been taking it easy ever since. They truly believe their work is done. It's reported this is where St Patrick spent his winters, designing the concept of Santa Claus.

Despite being a tiny place, everything has happened to Duleek except a nuclear event. Most people think this is due to the influx of people from Dublin. Several pubs and a TD's office in the village caught on fire in the last few years. Contrary to public opinion, nobody was at fault. The buildings in Duleek are just really accident-prone. Duleek also borders Drogheda and has a strong Republican presence in the area. Which is why everyone in Duleek loves going to Mass on Sundays. It's believed in five years' time Duleek will have its own Netflix documentary.

Duleek has a plethora of takeaways. One of them is called Little Naples, which is supposed to be a play on words but I don't want to have to imagine a place in Italy when I'm busy thinking about nipples. On a side note, the pizza is great.

People from Duleek really love tarmac. There are 4,000 people living in Duleek and 6,000 tarmac companies. This means that on average every man, woman and child owns 1.5 tarmac companies.

Beo is a coffee shop in Duleek. 'Beo' is Irish for 'alive', which I'm glad to hear, because the minimum I require from staff when I'm experiencing a coffee shop is a beating pulse. Beo is home to some of the best pastries in Meath. This coffee shop is a landing strip for people who stop in for a quick piss on the road to Belfast. When they start eating the sausage rolls, they sell the Nissan Micra they arrived in on and move to the village for good.

## Stamullen

Stamullen is a small village on the border of Meath. People often overlook Stamullen, but I believe it has a lot of redeeming qualities. It's such a small village that if you're an attention-seeker who needs constant drama and validation, if you so much as cross the road at the wrong time everyone in Stamullen will be talking about it for weeks. This is easy to do, because Stamullen doesn't believe in the concept of traffic lights.

### Urban myths and legends

Stamullen is basically a giant horse farm. Not really, but it sounds like it should be with a name like that. The forest in Stamullen has a certain spiritual quality to it. A social process occurs within its realm known as GAAtrification, a phenomenon that causes you to love playing football. It's rumoured the local GAA team that played there were all just friends who got lost in the forest and never made it out.

Stamullen has about five shops in it and 60 per cent of them are hairdressers. This is as it should be in a remote village. Everyone's hair grows much quicker when there isn't much else to do. There's even a special tournament hosted in the village each year called the Stamullen Hair Fair. This is a competition between the locals seeing who can grow their hair quicker within a 20-minute period. This game usually involves a referee using a measuring tape and a stopwatch, along with a strangely upbeat crowd. The same person wins every year, due to the fact that he's the only one who takes part. Everyone seems to be afraid of him so they just bask in his hair growth capabilities. He's known around the village as 'Stamullet'. He can grow 4 cm per day. He hasn't seen his family in years.

Another interesting artefact of Stamullen is the drive-thru chipper. It used to be a normal chipper but only became a drive-thru a few years ago when someone accidentally crashed into it. The driver of the car was greeted with excellent service and all the staff just acted like what happened was totally normal. They never made him feel weird about it. In fact, the driver even ordered a snack box and made himself feel at home, eating it before falling asleep in his car. The staff let him stay in his car for two weeks until he had to go to the toilet. This chipper has had an open-door policy ever since the door was ripped off its hinges.

Namaste.

# Kells

Kells is a town in County Meath. It's famous for being the main inspiration behind the Book of Kells, which is a book about Kells that was so boring they had it kept behind a glass case 70 km away in Trinity College. Some believe Kells only exists on the front of a 109 Bus Éireann bus from Dublin. Nobody ever stays on long enough to check if Kells is a real place. It's not worth the disappointment.

## Urban myths and legends

During 2019 the ATM in Kells was twice pulled out of the wall. Some would say this was due to a lone antagonist trying to rob from the bank, but it's really just because the ATMs in Kells are actually made out of jelly. How could you blame someone for robbing it, it's just so stealable! The bandits of the ATM in Kells never stole the money for selfish purposes, they believed in equal distribution of the wealth and after listening to the first five minutes of *The Communist Manifesto* in audiobook form, they got the gist of it and decided to take matters into their own hands.

Kells is surprisingly world-renowned for teaching the English language to Spanish students. In fact, Xabi Alonso arrived here as a teenager to learn English. He failed miserably. He didn't learn anything new in Kells because no one here speaks to each other in sentences longer than a one-syllable grunt.

There is a monastic site in Kells that has gained popularity amongst people who love being constantly reminded of death. It's a great place to visit if you love graveyards. Some say if you travel into this pit of darkness just before the break of dawn you'll see nothing. It's pitch black, what are you doing here?

## NIGHTLIFE

All the young adults of Kells used to go to The Vibe, a famous nightclub in the town. The Vibe was a hub of rural fun for young and old. You could often find a group of first-year college students beside ageing locals in sweaty unbuttoned dress shirts screaming in the DJ's ear to play 'Wagon Wheel' before his son comes in and finds out he's drinking again. The Vibe got its name due to the vibrational field around the nightclub. It was so magnetic that people from Navan wearing earrings were getting stuck to the door so the Vibe had to dial it down a bit, and now they only open on bank holidays weekends. Which works for everyone, because on bank holiday weekends people from Navan are too drunk to leave their house anyway.

Namaste.

## Ashbourne

Ashbourne is a commuter town on the long finger of the Greater Dublin Area, which is just another way of saying it's in Meath without having to adjust the prices to reflect the fact that if the electricity went off all you'd hear is cows mooing and farmers penetrating goats. Ashbourne was a settlement dating back to the Neolithic period. It was a defensive structure built to protect people who got overly sensitive when you told them wearing tracksuits and hanging around outside McDonald's all day doesn't necessarily make you a hardened criminal. Ashbourne is similar to the Bebo algorithim: dead. Although the town is abuzz with infrastructure and amenities, you never see anyone leave their house. Ashbourne is a ghost town, an undiscovered terrain filled with surprises and a Tesco that's so big you could fit all of your life's regrets in the frozen food section.

## Urban myths and legends

Perhaps the most sacred of Ashbourne's outdoor drinking temples is the weir. The weir is a big park in the middle of Ashbourne. The weir attracts locals with inner-city Dublin accents, yet, the luscious exterior of the park reminds them not to go too far on that electric scooter as they are still very much in Meath. The weir is where many ancient battles take place, usually between Ashbourne and everyone else. It's also where virginity goes to die.

On the topic of death: there is a statue in the middle of Ashbourne to commemorate the lives of the soldiers who fought in the 1916 rising. But because everyone in Ashbourne has such a short attention span, the only 1916 they know is the time on a digital clock. 1916 – also known as the time they smoke their second last joint of the evening. As a result, this statue has become known simply as 'the statue'. It's believed once all the pubs shut down on a Saturday night if you scratch the bottom of the statue with a two-euro coin it will chip the paint and you'll see a vision of local Ashbourne blow-in Johnny Logan playing *Grand Theft Auto* and avoiding responsibilities. He will look at you and beg that you tell no one you saw him here. You don't.

### NIGHTLIFE

Many Ashbourne natives have told me there is an unbearable pull towards Fogarty's nightclub at the end of a night out in the town. This is where everyone ends up when the pubs close. Everyone, even people that don't exist. They all congregate in Fogarty's and pretend to not secretly love everything about the place.

The other pubs in the area are all waiting rooms for the real main event of Ashourne, the San Remo chipper, a colosseum of battered sausages and salted, vinegary chips. Outside San Remo's you'll find the spectators drooling on their kebabs as they wait for the Ashbourne gladiators to engage in drunken battle. Which is usually known as the 'two S's'; shouting and shoving.

Namaste.

# COUNTY MONAGHAN

People have asked 'could Monaghan be Ireland's most underrated county?' And the answer is a resounding 'no'. Monaghan is rated exactly how it's deserved. Monaghan is a county, and that's about as far as you can truthfully go with it.

# Top five things you don't want to miss:

### 1. Carrickmacross lace
Monaghan is famous for the ancient Irish craft of lacemaking. These craftspeople are known as lacists. They don't know how to speak Irish or English. All they do is look at their shoelaces and drool.

### 2. Getting lost in a forest
Experience the unadulterated thrill of getting poached by Monaghanians in the wild. Watch their confused expressions as they poke you with a stick

### 3. Pointing out how Patrick Kavanagh is from Monaghan but no one from here knows how to read
And then quickly avail of the bypass that leads out of Monaghan town as the locals chase you with pitchforks.

### 4. Driving through it while closing your eyes so you don't have to see anything

### 5. Bog snorkelling
A famous tradition in Monaghan culture. Everyone in Monaghan is born to be a bog snorkeller and judging by their personality, it really shows.

## TOXICITY RATING: 9.7

# Clones

Clones is a small town in Monaghan. The most interesting thing that ever happened here was the invasion of the Normans, a group of substitute teachers named Norman who came to Clones and wore cardigans all throughout the summer because they were ashamed of their bodies. Pre-Christian Clones was a place of little importance, and with all the religious ruins in Clones today, it still is. The 'C' in Clones stands for consistency. Clones got its name because it's so small that everyone could be related. The people of Clones don't believe in the concept of procreation. Instead they take a strand of DNA and replicate themselves. If growth keeps up at its current rate, Clones will soon become the biggest empire in the world. And it'll be so weird.

## What you'll find here

Make sure to pop over to the round tower. This round tower is the oldest in Ireland, some say it was built in the tenth century by Bob Geldof. There's no roof on the round tower any more, which makes it look like a circumcised penis. Still noted as Bob Geldof's biggest contribution to society. Thanks for that, Bob.

When leaving the round tower, why not take a visit to St Tighearnach's abbey? It's basically just a graveyard. Truly capturing the essence of what Clones is all about. There are pirate symbols on the headstones in this cemetery. It turns out they're fake though. If you were a pirate, you wouldn't be in Monaghan.

Drop in to the Masonic temple in the town. The Freemasons have been in Clones since 1800. Contrary to popular belief, Freemasons aren't the secret society that controls the world. Their basic precepts are 'Brotherly love, relief and truth', which is why many Freemasons eventually come clean to their wives and admit they were using Grindr to cheat on them with lads who drive tractors.

Other than visiting religious sites, all there really is to do in Clones is keep walking. If you put one foot in front of the other your head won't catch up with you. This will stop you from coming to terms with what your life has become, and also, accepting the fact that no taxi has ever driven through here since the turn of the millennium.

## *NIGHTLIFE*

Once you've finished going on your panic-induced walk of Clones, make sure to go explore a taste of Clones nightlife in Packie Willies pub. Packie's is a favourite of the locals. The staff are very accommodating to outsiders, but only if they've walked before going to the pub. An intercom goes off every time a newcomer walks through the door, ordering them to reveal their Fitbit to the nearest barman before ordering a pint.

Other than that, sorry, no. Try Monaghan town.

Namaste.

# COUNTY OFFALY

Offaly is a total swamp. Offaly is a cousin you only see like once a year and when you go to his house for Christmas, you suddenly remember why you hate him so much. Offaly doesn't get any of your jokes and wants to talk about cancel culture because he watches too much American TV. The people of Offaly are known as BIFFOs. While it's believed that this is an acronym that means 'Big Ignorant Fucker From Offaly' it actually means 'Bogs In Fields Fulla Oldmen'.

# Top five things you don't want to miss:

## 1. Seasonal depression

In Offaly, they don't call it being down in the dumps, it's being beneath in the bog.

## 2. Eating Pringles in the rain at the ancient monastic site of Clonmacnoise

If you're in Offaly, definitely make sure you give this a go! You will scare tourists and tour guides alike with your strange behaviour, leaving them wondering why you're eating Pringles in the rain.

## 3. Walking through Tullamore and every time you see a car with an Offaly-reg plate, shouting 'OY!'

Nobody will know what you're screaming about but you will feel a tremendous sense of secret power.

## 4. The stampede to get into Melba's in Birr on a Saturday night

Every weekend the streets of Birr get infested with drunk Offalians trying to rush into Melba's so they can go to a night-club that almost makes them forget that they are still in Birr. There also appears to be a leakage of people from the community of North Tipperary and its surrounding environs. Because in North Tipperary, they have to travel all the way to Offaly just to get running water.

## 5. Small-town syndrome

This is an observable characteristic of the young Offalians. Small-town syndrome is when an individual (or often a group) is acting out in an egotistical way until someone finds out they're from Banagher or somewhere else equally as random. Once their true identity is revealed, the individual shrivels down to the size of a pea and a five-a-side team from Tullamore play football with them.

## TOXICITY RATING: 8.7

# Tullamore

Tullamore is the county town of Offaly. Massaged halfway between Dublin and Galway, Tullamore is the geographical bullseye of Ireland, bang smack in the middle of nowhere. Tullamore is a commuter town and the locals only go there to sleep and wait till it's time to go to work in Dublin again.

## Urban myths and legends

In 1785 Tullamore was notoriously remembered as being victim of the first hot air balloon incident, in which a hot air balloon fell in the town and caused a fire that destroyed about 130 homes. This begs the question, why would anyone want to fly over Tullamore in a hot air balloon?

The ICM is a cinema in Tullamore which was visited by Kanye West and Kim Kardashian for their honeymoon a few years ago. Although this cinema seems like a humble establishment, a theatre much like you'd find anywhere else, there's a secret room in there that shows movies of your future along with the soundtrack of the new Kanye album, whether you like it or not. Rumours suggest this is why Kanye and Kim went there in the first place, in the midst of this peculiar arrangement, the workers at the ICM made a carbon copy of this famous couple and the real Kim and Kanye work in this magical cinema now, they just gave them different name tags.

Tullamore Dew is the most popular beverage in Tullamore when you don't count the other beverages that are far more popular, such as water and tea. This ethereal broth is the most delicious drink known to man and upon its consumption the people of Tullamore actually start flying, which is why on a Saturday night, you'll see pot-bellied middle-aged men in their early 20s flying above your head in Offaly jerseys.

## *NIGHTLIFE*

The Palace is the pride and joy of Tullamore. This club attracts a young hip crowd who flock from across the country because apparently Darude played here once.

There is a taxi station in the area that's open 24/7. Only because people stand outside it and don't go in. Outside anywhere is open 24/7. This taxi station is the place where the drunken party people of Tullamore flock after a night out in the Palace, to stand there and play tunes on their Android phone until someone asks them to leave.

Namaste.

# COUNTY ROSCOMMON

Due to the lack of personality in the Roscommon people, Roscommon is simply known for its lakes. Because lakes can't screw things up, they're just there.

# Top five things you don't want to miss:

### 1. There's a circus elephant buried in Castlerea.
But because Castlerea are too afraid to go to the circus, they will never know she's there.

### 2. Sheep
The sheep here are also known as the forbidden temptation of Roscommon testosterone.

### 3. Scary builders
The builders in hi-vis jackets out here are a little bit rough around the edges, due to the harsh realities of acclimatising to the trauma of living in Roscommon. These construction workers are so intimidating that they are the reason Chris O'Dowd fled from Roscommon and became a famous actor.

### 4. Golf courses
Roscommon built millions of golf courses just so you could get a bit of space between yourself and the rest of the boring people who live here.

### 5. Asking the bouncers in Infinity how to conceptualise infinity
If you ask a bouncer about numerical data that doesn't include star signs they will get violent and start viciously swinging.

## TOXICITY RATING: 9.7

# Roscommon town

Roscommon town might actually be the only place in Roscommon, and it's barely even there. Roscommon town is a bit like Lapland, because it's only busy at Christmas. The rest of the year the only activity you see in the town is a stampede of young people running with their luggage to the nearest airport to emigrate to Australia, which is about as far away from Roscommon as you can ever get. Roscommon has loads of hills, which makes it a great choice for people who strongly dislike safety and warmth. Roscommon is the centre of business in Ireland, when you leave out Dublin, Galway, Cork and pretty much everywhere else. Roscommon is the perfect place to get a job. But only if you want to work in a bookie's, Supermac's or Castlerea Prison.

## Urban myths and legends

Roscommon has a higher population of lambs per capita than anywhere else in the country. This isn't because Roscommon is full of farmers, it's due to RLPT (Roscommon Lamb Progression Theory). RLPT was a theory invented by a scientist from Carlow years ago to explain why there are so many lambs. It's believed that when someone from Roscommon dies, their consciousness survives and they become a lamb. This lamb eventually turns into a sheep and the sheep turns into a Roscommon native. This theory explains why no one from Roscommon ever has anything interesting to say, and they usually just stand there, staring into space with their mouthes half-open, munching on a wet patch of grass. Roscommon even hosts a lamb festival every year. The locals get a bit too obsessed with the competition. Many of the Roscommon natives don't know that when they go to the festival to support the lambs, really they are holding up a mirror to themselves, their brothers, sisters and mortality.

Roscommon is well served by McNeill's, a local newsagent's. It's believed the deli in here was the first place the Roscommon natives ever tasted curry. They loved it, and when Roscommon natives get excited, it's terrifying! When the school day finishes the shop can get swamped with kids who flock to buy their beloved Kandee ketchup roll for two euro. The ketchup in these rolls often paint the streets of Roscommon blood red, which makes tourists think Roscommon is a violent town, but it's not. They're just a bunch of messy eaters.

My research has revealed that Roscommon isn't real. It's a figment in the imagination of local hero/barber Paddy Joe Burke. Paddy just kept saying 'Rossies' over and over somewhere in between Leitrim and

Longford until everyone forgot what words meant and fell under his spell and now they all think they live in Roscommon. Rosscommon is a collective hallucination, and until the day Paddy Joe Burke stops sleeping in his county colours, the natives of Roscommon will never be emancipated.

## *NIGHTLIFE*

Go to bed. Nothing to do here.
Namaste.

# COUNTY SLIGO

Sligo is baffling. Everyone who moves to Dublin from Sligo is a pre-packaged creative arts student with a drinking problem. And everyone else in Sligo, also has a drinking problem. Sometimes the small minority of people from Mayo who aren't delusional about how good Mayo is will pretend to be from Sligo for extra social capital, but they usually give themselves away, because if they were really from Sligo, they would have a strained relationship with their parents.

## Top five things you don't want to miss:

### 1. Visiting the local clown college
The local clown college is also known as Sligo IT. It used to be called Sluggo IT because if someone from there wakes up earlier than 2 p.m. they are considered a success.

### 2. The local obsession with W.B. Yeats
Yes, famous playwright William Butler Yeats hails from Sligo. And even though no one from Sligo is familiar with his work, they still love him.

### 3. The Strandhill-Rosses Point evolution
Strandhill is full of rich surfers and wine-drunk yummy mummies. If they can manage to hold on to their money they will eventually emigrate to Rosses Point, where the real rich people live, although they will never be truly accepted here unless they're a landlord.

### 4. Getting lost in the Quayside shopping centre
Why are there steps everywhere? Steps upstairs, steps downstairs, steps leading to fake doors, steps going up the wall. This was all done to trap outsiders in Sligo until they give up and start a new life here.

### 5. Cranmore vs The Hill
In Sligo town, the ancient battle between Cranmore and The Hill still wages on. Both trying to claim dominance over the big Dunnes, while the little Dunnes lays fallow waiting to be entered. Until the day the people of Cranmore can stop fighting with the people of The Hill for a parking space in Tesco carpark, there can never be peace in Sligo town.

**TOXICITY RATING: 7.1**

# Enniscrone

Enniscrone is a seaside town in County Sligo. It's a small village in the lap of wintery desolation. However, for a few months in the summer, Enniscrone comes to life through tourist rejuvenation. Outsiders flock here armed with a thick ratio of chunky cameras and winding maps that lead to nowhere. The locals of Enniscrone have been torn over the place name of their hometown, often calling it 'Inishcrone' or 'Iniscrone' because people from Enniscrone can't spell Enniscrone.

## What you'll find here

Enniscrone beach is one of the most picturesque beaches in the country. Some say there is a splinter organisation known as the Anti-Sligo Movement that socially engineered the beach to be a beacon of hope for everything Sligo stands against: beaches. This beach is completely out of place and due to a phenomenon known as the Diderot effect (look it up, no time to explain) it makes the rest of the county look like even more of a dump than it already is. It's believed the beach in Enniscrone stretches as far as the eye can see. No one has ever dared walk the path in its entirety. Once dusk settles over this foggy town, a conveyor belt opens up that goes from one stretch of the beach to the other and until the sun rises and the first pair of eyes glimpse the ocean, Enniscrone, to all intents and purposes, turns into the Caribbean.

When visiting Enniscrone make sure to pop into the Waterpoint Aqua Park. It's a fun day out for all the family, so if you plan on coming alone, don't. Just hire a fake family to come with you so you don't look like a creep going up the slides by yourself. If you were to untangle all the water slides and stretch them into a straight line they would bring you on a one-way path into a better place, Castlebar. Waterpoint got its name due to the temperature in the swimming pool where the water point is below freezing.

A few years ago a man decided to land a Boeing 747 in the middle of Enniscrone and hollow out the plane to rent it out for holiday accommodation. Unfortunately what ended up happening is, the man learnt how to fly from instructional YouTube videos and soon realised he didn't need to be in Enniscrone anymore. The only thing getting between him and Enniscrone was his lack of aviation experience.

Namaste.

# COUNTY TIPPERARY

Elegance, class and grace. These are three words that have nothing to do with Tipperary. Tipperary is a plantation of cows, hills and farmers that live in fear of Cork getting mad and shouting at them. Tipperary is a mirage. It seems promising from a distance, but as you get closer all hope disappears.

# Top five things you don't want to miss:

## 1. Bulmers
Go down to Clonmel and every time you hear a local even HINT at mentioning how cider is made here, stick an apple in their mouth before drop-and-rolling your way out of their personal space and into safety.

## 2. The Great Wall of Tipperary
The Great Wall of Tipperary is a mental construct. It marks the divide between Tipperary North and Tipperary South. They don't ever talk to each other. No one from the South has ever dared travel further north than Thurles, in fear that they might get bored to death.

## 3. Hurling
Tipperary is the home of hurling. It was invented in a hotel back in the 1800s when a group of men started beating each other with sticks for sexual pleasure. Then they had the idea to make it into a sport to hide the struggle with their sexuality and make it look like they were athletic.

## 4. Talking to the forgotten adults of Feile '94
Go to any pub in Tipp to see a man in his late 40s dressed like he's an extra in *Human Traffic*, or a woman who looks like a psychic healer and smells like ketamine. You can spot the forgotten adults of Feile '94 from a mile away because they'll start talking to you about the time Rage Against the Machine played in Tipperary about thirty years ago like it was the last time they ever experienced joy.

## 5. Manure
Come on down to Tipperary if you want to experience manure up close and personal.

**TOXICITY RATING: 8.9**

# Nenagh

Nenagh is the county town of Tipperary. It's also a really unfortunate girl's name. According to popular tourism website Ireland Before You Die, Nenagh was recently named the second-friendliest place in Ireland. Swords came in fourth place, which obviously means they just picked the places at random. Allegedly by encouraging a blindfolded intern to throw darts at a map.

## Urban myths and legends

Nenagh Castle is the oldest building in Nenagh. It was built in the thirteenth century, in the same year Brian McFadden put out his greatest hits album. The town of Nenagh was built around this castle. The inhabitants of Nenagh suffer from a gravely medieval malady where they get the unshakeable feeling that someone is going to shoot an arrow into their neck while walking through the town for crimes their ancestors' committed, maybe Brian McFadden.

The Junior B hurlers have wreaked havoc upon the Nenaghian ecosystem ever since time began. They stand up on pub chairs chanting hurling songs, as well as stealing all the potential female partners in the locality. This is why if you don't play hurling in Nenagh, you'll have to move to Limerick or die alone.

Mama's is a pizzeria where people go to eat because no one from Nenagh has parents. Before Mama's the concept of pizza in Tipperary was laughable. They used to have roast dinners every day of the week because it was all anyone knew how to cook. It's believed if you go into Mama's with a sad look on your face, Mama herself will appear in front of you and ask you where you see yourself in five years, before giving you a hug and sending you out into the wild to fend for yourself until you come thrashing back in here to inhale a family-sized pizza in one sitting.

# Cahir

Cahir is a small town in County Tipperary famous for its historical mysteries. It's a well-known resting place for Americans who want to find out about their ancestry. They usually find it incredibly difficult to spend more than one evening in Cahir, seeing as there is nothing to do. It's a one-night pit stop on the rambling road to Cork City. Part of the reason for this passive tourism is due to the fact that Cahir is on the Limerick–Waterford railway line. The trains only come twice a day. On Sundays, the train doesn't come at all. Some believe this is because of the traditional values Cahir still holds close, although it's actually because on Sundays, Cahir ceases to exist. There are only six days of the week in Cahir. This makes the locals look about one-seventh younger than they actually are and infinitely more disappointed. If you drink from the fountain of youth, there are better places to do it than in Cahir.

## Urban myths and legends

Some say if you go to Cahir Castle in the summer and wear a tracksuit, it acts as an invisibility cloak and hides you away from all the tourists who flock there once the sun is out. This is because an Irish person wearing a tracksuit doesn't fit into their cultural narrative of what it means to be Irish. This isn't something to be upset about. When do you ever get the opportunity to zoom around and pretend to be a ghost without someone thinking you're weird?

Another historical monument lies in direct opposition to the neighbouring Rock of Cashel; it's called the Pebble of Cahir, erected by the county council in 1992. It's an unassuming stone made out of solidified sighs of the locals who are bored of Cahir. If you throw it hard enough against a wet wall it has the power to make paint dry.

If you plan on leaving no stone unturned, make sure to pay a visit to the Swiss Cottage, a mystery unto itself. It's a giant fortress that looks like something Shrek would live in. It's by far the biggest cottage I've ever seen. It makes you feel like you took the wrong pill and entered into a Tipperary reboot of Alice in Wonderland. The Swiss Cottage is a great place to go if you like feeling really small.

## NIGHTLIFE

Cahir has an incredibly rich nightlife. Although it's not due to any particular social events or anything worthwhile happening here. At night time the men of Cahir undergo a drastic personality change after drinking four cans of Bulmers Berry. They put on a superhero costume and pretend to be from Clonmel. The Cahir men convince themselves they are fighting crime and evil forces that keep Cahir trapped in the ever-looming shadow of Cork City, but because there is no crime or evil forces holding Cahir down, they usually just end up fighting amongst themselves, often to the disappointed glances of disheartened American tourists who came here to explore their heritage.

Namaste.

## Goatenbridge

Goatenbridge is a scenic village in the middle of County Tipperary. Goatenbridge got its name because there's a goat on the bridge that won't move in case a farmer turns him into a coat. The locals then decided to call it Goatenbridge because everyone in Tipperary speaks really fast without taking any breaths in between their words. Goatenbridge is barely even a real place. It's more of a crossroads within rural Munster. A crossroads between 'Why am I in Tipperary?' and 'What am I doing with my life?'

## Urban myths and legends

It's believed that underneath the bridge lies the River Tar. This has confused scientists for centuries. Now it's safe to assume the tar ended up in the river because there was an oil spill in Thurles and nobody bothered to clean it up.

If planning a getaway to Goatenbridge, make sure to pack plenty of clothes as the locals will haggle you for the shirt on your back due to the lack of shops here. In fact, a man in a van delivers groceries around the area from the nearest Tesco, 30 minutes away.

All of the great work in Goatenbridge is conducted by people in vans. Which leads to the mysterious question on everybody's lips: what happened to the chipper van that landed in Goatenbridge from Thursday to Sunday? I can now confirm that Goatenbridgers (the locals) experience a collective hallucination once halfway through the week and suffer from the delusion that a man hands them chips in a bag. It never happened. Nobody in Goatenbridge has ever seen a van.

A mountain range overlooks Goatenbridge, the mountains of Knockmealdown. Knockmealdown mountain is a safari park for the unadventurous. It's a great place to go if you love the colour green and love the texture of wet grass and depression. Knockmealdown got its name because the goddess of Goatenbridge, known as Goatenbridgess, used to knock meals down from the top of the mountain straight into the grateful mouths of the Goatenbridge people, due to their lack of restaurants. They were microwave meals, piping hot. The only place it's safe to use a microwave in Goatenbridge is at the top of the mountain. Ground-level microwaves are far too much responsibility.

When visiting Goatenbridge, make sure you explore the Liam Lynch Monument. This is a memorial that commemorates where Irish Republican Liam Lynch got shot in 1923. The statue doesn't look like Liam Lynch, it looks more like a giant, erect stone penis. A strange observation one may notice at this monument is that it only gets erect when people are looking at it. It's an exhibition piece. The opposite of stage fright.

## NIGHTLIFE

Exploring the nightlife in Goatenbridge is a rather one-dimensional process. The monopoly on the social life of Goatenbridge is run by Glen View, the only bar in the village. This bar is frequented by the locals as a safe space to listen to upbeat music on a speaker. In fact, the jukebox has been through more hands than the water feature in Lourdes. The mystery of Glen View is nobody has ever seen this mysterious 'Glen' because he is invisible. Some say he just loves sitting there enjoying the atmosphere of the Goatenbridge ecosystem in uninterrupted peace. Namaste.

## Thurles

Thurles is in geographical limbo. The interesting fact about this small town is that if you hate it here, it'll take you ages to escape because it's bang smack in the middle of the county. As a result, nobody ever really leaves Thurles. The grass is always such an effort on the other side. Thurles was historically an agricultural town. It still is, but because they built a Supervalu and a Lidl they now have the audacity to call themselves a retail centre.

### Urban myths and legends

Semple Stadium is the pride and joy of Thurles. It is the breeding ground of the GAA lifestyle. All children of Thurles have to undergo an ancient ritual where they attempt to balance a sliotar on a hurl for three seconds. If they drop it, they get thrown into the River Suir. The children that grow up to survive this traumatic ceremony inevitably found themselves back at the Feile festival in the same stadium between 1990 and 1997. Usually looking for their jaws and ignoring phone calls from their worried parents, who they haven't seen since they threw them in the river all those years ago. The legend about Feile is that if you say 'Yup Thurles' three times at a local afterparty, a lad in his 40s will walk in through the kitchen window and talk about how great the pills were at Feile and how no one understands music these days.

Hayes Hotel is a central talking point of the Thurles lifestyle. This is where the GAA was invented. This has led to an influx of tourists from Ohio wandering in and asking the staff if GAA is another form of soccer. Hayes didn't mean to create the GAA, lads in tight shorts running into each other and pretending to care about a football was just a kink that got out of hand.

The young adult males of Thurles only have an interest in doing two things: chatting up French students in the car park or swimming out in Lady's Well. These two ancient pastimes are usually accompanied with copious amounts of alcohol, to bestow confidence upon the Thurles natives. Nobody knows why there are French students in Thurles to begin with. Some argue that they are here by mistake. They got washed up on the shore on the way to Cork.

### NIGHTLIFE

Hayes Hotel nightclub is the main watering hole of the Thurles people. It attracts a young, adventurous crowd who like talking about GAA. It's believed you're not allowed in unless you're wearing a county jersey. The ancient myth states that if you go out to the smoking area in this club and say the words 'Haze us bejaysus' a 45-year-old man appears at the bar trying to get social approval off the 20-year-olds, in a desperate attempt to relive his glory days. He soon gets whisked away by the bouncers. Last week he got so drunk that he threatened to glass someone. He was looking in the mirror. At home. Namaste.

## Tipperary town

Tipperary town is a town in Tipperary, because Tipperary loves naming itself after itself, and hates creativity. Tipp town is situated on the River Ara, if you swim in the river when no one is watching the river will bring you towards a slowboat full of Cork City heads, but they squawk so loudly that you'll drown yourself to stop hearing their bird-like screeching. Tipp town is a farming community; the cows control the farmers through rapid eye movement sensors. These microchipped farmers have become non-playable characters in the video game of Irish Dairy.

## Urban myths and legends

Tipp town plaza was the most interesting thing to ever happen to the town. Even though the plaza is really just a big petrol station with a Supermac's inside it. The plaza is where custom wheels and trance tunes from the '90s unite as one. This is the temporary temple of the boy racer. They stay here as long as it takes for them to get ejected by the security guard. The plaza is in the process of developing a conveyor belt that empties trays of chilli cheese chips directly into your mouth.

The roads of Tipp town are paved with good intentions, but mostly potholes, and the road eventually leads to Thurles, so no one ever drives on it just in case they end up really bored. When entering the realm of Tipp town, be sure to ask the locals about the mysterious bypass the government have been promising them for years, if you want to make them sad.

Make sure to visit the historical monument in the centre. It's a bronze statue of a man called Charles Kickham. No one in Tipperary knows who he is, but we can only assume he was a really good footballer. When a statue man gets erected in Tipp town, the locals don't question it, in fear that someone will make a statue out of them too.

Years ago, Tipp town was a military barracks for the British army. You could say that Tipp town went from being the home of the black and tans to being the home of lads in fake tan who will eventually go on a J1 to California and settle on moving up to Dublin once they realise they'll never make it on to *Love Island*.

### NIGHTLIFE

Like most places in Ireland, the nightclubs in Tipp town are not nightclubs, but if you want to call the pubs night-clubs, fine, go ahead.

Kiely's is the best nightclub in Tipp town. Make sure to avail of their fantastic carvery lunch during the day, and at night, reports suggest you can have the time of your life at Kiely's which turns into a Supermac's/ice skating rink with country music playing in the background while no one's looking. Allegedly, Garth Brooks showed up here one night and bathed in a tub of Guinness but nobody recognised him because he was naked.

Namaste.

# COUNTY TYRONE

Tyrone is a massive field. Some say Tyrone is the Laois of Ulster. Tyrone's main draw is their ancient stones. Which, much like the attitudes of the people, date back to the Bronze Age.

# Top five things you don't want to miss:

### 1. Beaghmore stone circles

This is a great place to go if you love staring at weird-looking stones that are just standing there in a field for no reason. People like to come here on a Sunday morning to pretend to feel a connection to our Celtic roots. Even though last night they were up until 5 a.m. pretending to feel a connection to their coke dealer's phone once they ran out and were forced to be sober.

### 2. Tim Horton's

Tim Horton's is a coffee-shop chain in Tyrone. When you get there, make sure to try the Ulster coffee. They say that once you drink it, you'll become hooked on *Britain's Got Talent* within a week.

### 3. Cookstown grungers

The Cookstown grungers are an interesting cohort of people. They are basically anyone from Cookstown who wears eyeliner. In Cookstown, this is seen as an act of social violence, as it is illegal to wear makeup here.

### 4. The blue pill

Take the blue pill in Tyrone. There is no start or end point. There are just fields upon endless fields. Tyrone is a faulty PlayStation 2 game. Every time you get as far as Omagh, you're pushed back to the last checkpoint of fields.

### 5. Taking a trip to Tomney's pub.

Tomney's is one of Tyrone's best-loved pubs. It's a great place to go if you like being confused into thinking you're in your granny's house. This delusion lulls you into a state of calm. The only difference between this place and where your granny lives is you don't have to stay sober enough here to operate the chairlift that pushes her up and down the stairs.

**TOXICITY RATING: 8.9**

# Omagh

Omagh is the county town of Tyrone. Omagh isn't real, it's actually a discontinued PlayStation 1 game about farmers. The Omaghians are well known to tend to the land, as Omagh consists mostly of agricultural communities. There may be no Wi-Fi here but a few weeks ago they found out rubbing rocks together can start a fire.

## Urban myths and legends

When visiting the realm of Omagh, make sure to sample some of the delicious cuisine that the town has to offer. Although it's important to note, the sandwiches of Omagh are segregated. There are two Subways. Catholic Subway and Protestant Subway. You can tell you're in Catholic Subway because the Wolfe Tones are playing on a loudspeaker and everyone keeps calling you *mo chara*. You'll know you're in a Protestant Subway because the customers can afford a foot-long meatball marinara without getting into a negotiation with the girl behind the till.

Omagh is where the rest of Tyrone and Fermanagh go to do their shopping. Unfortunately, when they get inside the shops, they don't know how money works so they just freeze in fear until they get asked to leave. Research suggests that some of the shops in Omagh aren't even real, they're just holographic representations of shops to lure people into thinking that Omagh can compete with Newry.

Like most other places that have nothing in it, the bus depot is one of Omagh's main attractions. The locals love it here, because it represents their only chance of escape. The bus depot is also where the young Omaghian's have their first kiss. Once this occurs they graduate to spending the rest of their adolescence hanging around outside the Iceland, which becomes their second home. These Omagh teenagers are generally peaceful, opting to spend their days talking about table linen. Once the youths pass through this phase of their development, they pass on to the next stage. They graduate from the car park of Iceland to spend the rest of their lives sitting outside Bob and Bert's. Bob and Bert's was a revolutionary forerunner in Omaghian lifestyle. This café brought coffee to the town. And ever since then, people from Omagh have awoken from their sleep walking fever dreams. Now they're awake, and even more dangerous.

## Dromore

Dromore is a small village in Tyrone. Dromore is the only place in Northern Ireland where the male population makes up 100 per cent of the entire community. Dromore is effectively a glorified men's shed for farmers, construction workers, footballers and old men who love to drink. Beware: the locals are incredibly keen to make you a citizen of Dromore. Some of them even stand outside the church and if you make eye contact with them they'll try to shake your hand and won't let go until you agree to join the parish.

### Urban myths and legends

Dromore is a fake village created by the GAA to store all of Northern Ireland's best footballers in close proximity. GAA is all Dromorians are ever allowed to talk about. Sometimes they talk about the weather too, but only if it's to do with the possibility of a match being cancelled on Sunday. On paper it would seem like GAA rules over Dromore with an iron fist. That's because it definitely does.

For a fake village, the amount of consumer choice in Dromore is astonishing. There are three whole shops! They have a Spar, a Vivo and John Kelly's newsagent. These are the only places that offer employment in Dromore. The fourth option would be standing in a bog somewhere waving at cars as they pass by. But you'll never find a job in Dromore doing that. Everyone does it, the market is flooded. Vivo have the best deli counter in the Dromorian ecosphere. They say the sausage, egg and bacon on soda bread can heal any hangover known to man. At least until the locals go to the off license and start drinking again, repeating the cycle over and over. The holy trinity in Vivo is the filled soda, twenty Benson and a can of Boost. If you're still feeling peckish for a takeaway in Dromore you might want to try out Swifdoh's. The pizza here is such good value that you can feed an entire family on a tenner. If you don't have a family, this is not your sign to start one now. Just come in by yourself, you freak.

## NIGHTLIFE

Surprisingly, yes! There are at least five pubs in Dromore. Which is a lot considering how few people live here. But when you realise the enormity of living in a secret fake village set up by the GAA, five pubs is nowhere near enough to numb the existential pain. The Central is one of the favourite pubs of the locals in Dromore. It's also the most generic name the GAA could think of when they were building the movie set of Dromore. It's a great place for a quiet pint, with friendly bar staff and great-value pricing. But make sure not to stay for too long. If they realise you don't like football it can get so quiet in there that you can hear your own thoughts. Inevitably, thoughts like 'how did I ever end up in Dromore?'

Namaste.

# COUNTY WATERFORD

Waterford is the session capital of Ireland. Every time you party with people from Waterford you almost die. People from Waterford are resilient, built to sustain the harshest of climates. Most people think it's because of their ancestry. Waterford city was the only place Cromwell didn't capture. But they actually just have a high tolerance to pain because they're used to handing over their hard-earned cash for a 1.8 g 50 bag.

# Top five things you don't want to miss:

### 1. Counting how many times you get called 'boss'

Everyone here thinks you're a boss and they'll let you know it. Unless, of course, you actually happen to be their real boss, in which case they will do everything in their power to make you believe they can't come into work because they've got Covid when in reality they were up necking Blue Ghosts all night. Which basically feels like the same thing.

### 2. Waterford Crystal

Waterford Crystal is known as a famous glass company, but it's also a catchphrase for a gang of three or more Waterfordians crowding around a bus stop, smoking meth.

### 3. The Battle of the Waterford Rock

For centuries, the Waterfordians and the Kilkennians have been engaging in a ruthless battle over who owns this massive rock that is obviously in Waterford. Because people from Kilkenny have poor spatial navigation skills and don't believe in boundaries, they think the rock is in Kilkenny, which is why they keep painting it yellow. This started a painting war with both counties painting their county colours over the rock. The victor of this majestic battle is yet to be confirmed, but it is believed to be the owner of the paint shop.

### 4. Telling a Waterford local that you can buy blaas in Lidl now

For years, Waterford have gained a sense of superiority over the rest of the country just because one of them knows how to bake their own bread from scratch. But whoever invented the blaa clearly had no idea how to spell. There's no need for the second 'a'. The baker was calling it a 'bla' and got distracted by his hatred of Kilkenny and couldn't remember if he put the first 'a' in it or not, which makes perfect sense, because everyone from Waterford suffers from short-term memory loss anyway. Now the recipe has been replicated and spread all over the country. If you remind a Waterfordian of this fact they will look at you like you just kicked their puppy.

5. Telling a student in Waterford IT that you are a being from the future that got sent here to tell them to drop out of their marketing degree and join the call centre like the rest of Waterford.

Oh no wait, never mind, they're doing it anyway.

## TOXICITY RATING: 8.4

## Tramore

Tramore is a scenic seaside town on the edge of Waterford. Tramore in Irish means 'big beach'. Which is essentially all Tramore really is. Despite this, Tramore is popular amongst tourists looking to experience the Irish lifestyle without paying for Dublin prices. Tramore is not to be confused with Traless, an inferior village that looks identical but is slightly sadder. Many Dubliners also flock to Tramore for their annual pilgrimage. They call it 'Marbheya'.

### Urban myths and legends

Some say Tramore is situated on a never-ending hill. Like many towns built on hills, the outline of Tramore itself is a physical representation of its social hierarchy. Reports suggest that the tourists and the common Tramoreians live at the bottom of the hill. This land is divided between the tour guides and the carnival workers, who compete against each other for resources. They live on a diet of ice cream, cotton candy and repressed anger towards the annoying kids they have to pretend to be nice to. The top of the hill is home to the wealthy socialites of Tramore. The landlord class. It can be hard to catch them in the wild because the only time they'll ever come down the hill is when they walk down far enough to get their entire mansion in a landscape photo on their smartphone.

Another legend of the Tramore ecosystem is the amusement park. While some say it's haunted, everyone agrees it's *at least* dangerous. At 3 a.m. you'll hear the muffled screams of tourists who were fed an Americanised ideal of what Ireland has to offer and got trapped in the popcorn machine so they couldn't write a TripAdvisor review and expose the truth. Once the screams stop if you step inside a bumper car and put a euro in it, it seperates from the machine and goes for a swim in the river.

Across the road from the amusement park lies Tramore beach. This is a beach made out of rocks and, possibly, human remains. This beach gets so overcrowded that many have tried to escape on a sunny day but there were so many people there that by the time they reached the exit, many years had passed and their life was over. Tramore beach is a place you should avoid on a sunny day, although the vultures seem to love it.

## NIGHTLIFE

The nightlife in Tramore is like nowhere else if you like being in bed by 11 p.m. The only place that's open after that is The Baldy Man bar. Some say being bald in Tramore is the highest honour Tramoreians can bestow upon themselves. People with long hair have to work on the Ferris wheel and are only allowed wash their hair in the sea once a week. Going bald eradicates the need for the Tramore natives to bathe themselves, due to the fact that people from Tramore don't really have sweat glands.

Namaste.

## Waterford city

Waterford city claims to be the oldest city in Ireland. Which is why everyone looks so tired of being here. In fact, it's all they ever talk about. Waterford is famous for its historical heritage, and for glorifying the Vikings, just because the Vikings cared enough about them to colonise them. Waterford has Stockholm syndrome on a widespread level. Everything in Waterford is on pause, while they wait in silent sadness for the fateful day they get colonised by lads with long hair again. Everyone in Waterford is colour-blind. Because Waterford is home to a local delicacy known as red lead, which isn't even red, it's purple, and it's basically glorified Billy Roll.

## Urban myths and legends

When visiting Waterford, make sure to pop into The Red Square, the hub of Waterford consumerism. Sit down on one of the benches and look at all the Waterfordians buzz by. The Red Square got its name because the path was paved in blood in a holy war about who invented the blaa, was it Waterford or Kilkenny? Needless to say nobody won, because the blaa is overrated.

The Spraoi Festival is an event run by the local theatre company every August bank holiday that celebrates the arts in Waterford. It's a great spectacle to see the talent that the city has to offer, but the most important part of this festival is the parade on the Sunday night that has been traumatising the local kids of Waterford ever since it began. This parade of terrifying characters is excellent for the character development of the children, who are forced to grow up quickly and face their fears vis-à-vis a grunting man in an ill-fitting monkey suit.

### NIGHTLIFE

Factory is the local nightclub where all the hipsters and art college students go to pretend to be really into tech-house music. It's also where the local GAA team go to get confused by the lack of Garth Brooks songs being played here.

For a more traditional Irish experience, head into Jack Meade's if you want to feel like you're breaking into someone's cottage. You'll be pleasantly surprised by the friendly staff and prompt service. If only all breaking and entries could be so pleasant, you'd probably stop stealing from your mother's purse and take your criminality out on the general public.

Namaste.

# COUNTY WESTMEATH

The government believed that Westmeath is the only county in Ireland that didn't deserve its own name. The other running title was 'JoeDolanistan'.

## Top five things you don't want to miss:

### 1. Exchanging your currency in Mullingar

Mullingar have their own currency in the town, known as the Gar. Hometown sweetheart Niall Horan has his face on the money. Before him, the face on the money belonged to Mullingar's second best singer, John Joe Nevin.

### 2. Having breakfast with Bressie

And as soon as you're settled in, he'll make you go for a run with him and read out motivational quotes from his phone to keep your spirits up. Oh no wait, those are his lyrics.

### 3. The Fleadh

The Fleadh Cheoil in Mullingar is a place where anxious kids with musical talent get to feel the vicarious social pressure of their parents' ambitions.

### 4. Observing the invasion of the yupbros on their way to Life Festival

The Monday after the festival ends, is said to be the real-life remake of the *Jaws* movie, except there's no shark and the jaws are all on the floor.

### 5. Pointing and laughing at the signpost for Moate

Why would you ever want to go to Moate? That'd be so weird.

## TOXICITY RATING: 9.2

# Mullingar

Mullingar is a large town in the Midlands, no one is really sure exactly where.

As soon as the sun rises in Mullingar, the sons of ex boy racers congregate in their fathers' Adidas tracksuits. They hang around the Market Square to spend the day loitering, comparing sleeve tattoos and saying things that don't really make sense such as 'Mullingar on top'. These adult children of the Market Square are very similar to pawns on a chessboard. They're only allowed move one step forward or diagonally. If they move any further, they'll no longer be in the Market Square, as it's essentially just a set of really slow traffic lights. Some of these natives are dispatched to the diving board. You can spot them out because they're the ones that never jump into the water. They're a holographic image and if they unzip their tracksuit everyone will see that they're a simulation of the Midlands adult male. A by-product of the Mullingarian imagination.

## Urban myths and legends

The females of Mullingar only exist in the perception of the Mullingar males. They begin to hallucinate, and think the statue of Joe Dolan is singing his hit single 'You're Such a Good Looking Woman' they start to get a mirage of Mullingar women wearing Westmeath jerseys and shouting at each other. These Mullingar natives don't exist outside daylight hours, once the moon falls over Mullingar, they disappear completely.

Another reason why I'd like to make the argument that Mullingar is not a real place, is the mere fact that their local park has a swimming pool in the middle of it. This would never happen in real life. Mullingar isn't a town, it's a glitch in a PlayStation 2 game. Parents often have to take that long walk of shame through the park towards the swimming pool with their children, walking past the spot they conceived them in. No one from Mullingar procreates in a bed. Everything is done outside these days.

### NIGHTLIFE

At night time, Dolan's pub becomes Mojo's nightclub, a cherished land of late-night debauchery. The floor here is so sticky that if you look at the soles of your runners after leaving the club, they've been stamped with the words *Thanks for coming to Mojo's, see you next weekend bai* written entirely out of chewing gum. Some say people just go to Mojo's to go to Lingus chipper afterwards and watch the late-night entertainment in the square. At night time the square becomes a coliseum where lads from Longford fight for dominance. Nobody ever gets too badly hurt, thanks to the spiritual master of Mullingar, Count Tornado. Count Tornado swoops down once the fight turns into physical contact, which rarely happens anyway, because people from the Midlands don't really fight, they just shout at each other until one of them walks away. Count Tornado falls out of the sky in his cape and his back-to-front keyboard, urging people to not throw rocks at his door. This lulls the unruly crowd into a state of relaxation. Because when push comes to shove, no one here really wants to fight each other. They're just frustrated the Lane Club is shut down and they have nowhere else to drink 2-euro vodka Redbulls.

Namaste.

## Kinnegad

Nestled in between the confused enclave of Meath and Westmeath lies the village of Kinnegad. The Battle of Kinnegad has been ongoing ever since the locals learnt how to use the internet. So the battle has been ongoing for roughly three weeks. Once upon a time, Kinnegad was a village of farmers who knew nothing of the world outside Westmeath. All of a sudden, swathes of folk from Clondalkin, Tallaght and Ballyfermot got lost and thought they were still in the west of Dublin so they set up shop in a field somewhere. Refusing to interact with the locals, because they were judging them. Another interesting fact about Kinnegad is that they have the highest percentage of cigarette smokers in the country, with over 120 per cent of the locals going through at least a pack a day. For years Kinnegad have been trying to gain autonomy from the rest of the country due to this fact alone, petitioning to be re-named as 'Kinnegad and Tobacco'.

## Urban myths and legends

When the council was in the middle of building Tesco and Aldi, it's alleged that the people of Kinnegad rallied against them in protest. The locals feared that these new additions might bring them one step closer to becoming a news story in one of those fake magazines that nobody reads with a headline that says something like 'Top 10 reasons you should consider a move to Kinnegad'.

Kinnegad used to be a stronghold of tired journey folk who made a stop-off in the village before travelling out west. This title was unfortunately stripped from them when the M4 motorway was built, meaning the people who now enter Kinnegad are all definitely there on purpose, not by convenience.

The GAA club in Kinnegad has a 60-ft tunnel underneath it that leads to an estate called Manorfield, but the Manorfieldians will never find out, because they're all from Dublin and no one from Dublin has ever played football.

### NIGHTLIFE

Most adventurers who used to travel into the realm of Kinnegad in the pre-M4 era inevitably landed in Harry's hotel. This was a resting place by day and by night it turned into a sugar club. This was the most famous nightclub in Kinnegad, unfortunately it had to get shut down because everyone kept licking the walls. The hotel had to rebuild the nightclub every Sunday morning after a big weekend, buying truckloads of sugar to recreate this palace of sweet dust. Overall, the sugar club became a real toothache for all involved.

Scanlon's is the loved watering hole of the Dubliners of Kinnegad. They also have arguably the best full Irish in the village. They tried it out by giving it to a group of American students and when they finished their breakfast they developed a Kinnegad accent and a visa. Scanlon's have a TV that only plays CCTV footage of the Spire on O'Connell street 24/7 to make their patrons feel more at home.

Namaste.

# COUNTY WEXFORD

Wexford is also known as the land where Dubs park their caravans. Wexford is a second home from home for the people of the capital. Places like Gorey and Courtown have been invaded over the last twenty years. And these Dublin families refuse to leave until the government build a Luas line that brings them all the way back to Santry.

# Top five things you don't want to miss:

## 1. The Centenary Stores
Go to the smoking area of the Stores, scoff as many handpicked strawberries as you can and see how long it takes for the bouncers to launch you out the front door.

The bouncers in the Stores are strawberry-detection robots, trained to catch strawberry eaters in the act and eject them with haste. The longest time on record is 3.76 seconds.

## 2. Shedfest
It's believed everytime you hear a Wexford girl say 'ye goin' to Shedfest hun?' another family from Dublin invade the area. Wexfordians believe this is Wexford's answer to Electric Picnic, but instead of Kendrick Lamar you just have the winner of the local battle of the bands and half the parish of New Ross.

## 3. Asking someone from Wexford town if a rissole and a battered burger are the same thing
This is something you don't want to miss out on when visiting Wexford town! But only if you don't value being alive.

## 4. The fairy of Ferndale
This is a great one for those of you that like magic! All you have to do is park your car in Ferndale and when you come back it'll either be missing, burnt out or the tyres will be customised with alloy plates. This was not the work of man, this was done by the fairy of Ferndale.

## 5. Experience the culture of Camolin
Camolin is the lonely little brother of Wexford. Camolin is very shy and self-conscious for having nothing in it. Camolin gets so excited when people stop by for refreshments, and is so disappointed when they realise they were only stopping by on the way to their final destination: Wicklow.

**TOXICITY RATING: 9.1**

# Wexford town

Wexford town is the county town of County Wexford. Wexford named the town after itself because it has the perfect mixture of narcissism and a fear of having a name that doesn't already exist. In Wexford town, there are only two types of people: Jacks and Marys. No interesting names allowed. Wexford is famous for being a Viking town. Many believe this is due to the Vikings settling here in 800 AD. In truth, it's just because everyone here has chest hair.

## Urban myths and legends

Some people argue that strawberries were invented in Wexford. Back in the 1800s raspberries were illegal and some Wexfordians tried to make bathtub raspberries to sell on the black market. They messed it up so badly that they accidentally created a strawberry, which was infinitely better anyway. Strawberries don't have hairs on them.

For some reason, most of Dublin tend to travel all the way down to Wexford for their summer holidays. Usually colonising the neighbouring areas of Rosslare, Blackwater, Curracloe and Courtown. This brings a lot of money into the economy of Wexford, while also making the place very loud, full of Wexfordians that hate everyone from Dublin for ruining their picturesque environment.

## Local cuisine

The rissole is the famous delicacy of Wexfordian life. It's basically a bunch of mashed-up chips, deep fried into a ball with oil and herbs. It's unique to the area so you can't get it anywhere else. Thankfully this virus hasn't spread further afield. The Wexfordians all agree this artery-clogging arte-fact shaves at least five years off the local life expectancy. They say it's a small price to pay. If they can knock a few years off having to listen to lads from Cabra talk about how Wexford is basically Dublin that's a chance that most of them are willing to take. The best rissoles in Wexford town are said to come from a chipper called The Premier. Which is where they magically grow on trees. The Premier doesn't have any staff there, because everyone in Wexford is on their holidays. Instead, they just leave a bucket at the door where residents pay for the rissole they pick off the in-house rissole tree, but they don't know what the bucket is there for, so they just end up getting sick into it instead.

## Enniscorthy

Enniscorthy is the second-largest town in Wexford. It's caught in the middle of the county, which means that Enniscorthy is a ham-fisted mix of south Wexford and Dublin invaders who play terrible music really loud on a broken boom box and constantly take their tops off because they think they're on holiday. Until Enniscorthy can give up the war and acknowledge that there is room for the influences of both north and south Wexford, Enniscorthy will never be at peace.

### Urban myths and legends

Enniscorthy natives are a proud bunch. Some would say their pride comes purely from the fact that they live in Enniscorthy and has little to do with accolades or accomplishments. People from Enniscorthy think they're too good for the English language and they're not bothered learning Irish, so they invented their own dialect. People from Enniscorthy are known as 'scalders'. Many are baffled when contemplating the origins of this phrase. It turns out the phrase comes from a ritual that each local has to partake in once they turn eighteen where they have to have a bath in boiling hot tea. They became scalders after they scalded themselves. Enniscalded.

Enniscorthy Castle has a fake ghost in the dungeon. The fake ghost has often appeared in ghost-hunter videos that look like they were recorded on a phone that doesn't even have a camera. This fake ghost is really friendly and it turns out so is the actor in real life. If you go into Enniscorthy castle when the paranormal activity winds down for the night you can see the fake ghost taking a bath and sobbing silently. He may be a fake ghost, but he is trapped in a real dungeon!

When visiting Enniscorthy, take a trip to the Secret Valley Wildlife Park. This is where all the unruly Dubs who misbehave themselves in Courtown get sent to spend the rest of their holiday in captivity.

## NIGHTLIFE

Benedict's is the main nightclub in Enniscorthy. This place has a carnival vibe to it, but once you get there, in your usual desolate drunken state, you find the only clown there is you. At the centre of the Benedict's dancefloor hangs a beautiful chandelier. Many have become lost to the precious glow of the chandelier over the years. Some say this chandelier is put there to distract the audience so that they don't notice the fake ghost of Enniscorthy castle sneaking up behind you asking you how you like your eggs before cracking one over your head and shouting 'Benedict!'

Namaste.

## New Ross

New Ross is a small town in the south of Wexford. It's famous for its picturesque old buildings, even though it's basically just Navan in technicolour. New Ross is situated along the River Barrow. Many like to go swimming in this river before going to work, so that when they show up to work they smell like river. New Ross used to be Old Ross, but nobody liked Old Ross so he had to change his personality. Many have walked past the big statue in the town and wondered why it's there. The common answer was that the statue commemorates the lives lost in the 1798 rebellion, but it's really just put there to keep the people of New Ross in a state of confusion, preventing them from getting any work done.

## Urban myths and legends

New Ross is home to a replica Famine ship. Make sure to jump on board for the Famine ship experience: you'll see really healthy-looking actors playing sick, hungry Irish people, but at least they do their best to starve you while you're there. They don't even have biscuits. Reports suggest if you go on board with a pack of crisps, it will create a glitch in the simulation and it will push the entire country back into 1847, except instead of British planters, the oppressors are now a half-empty sentient bag of crisps crinkling in the wind.

New Ross has a rich affinity with the arts. Make sure to catch a show at St Michael's theatre when you get here. This theatre hosts 300 events per year and it's the only place where real life exists. The show really starts when you walk through New Ross and you think everything is real. The stage is the one true reality in New Ross. The actors are caught in a misunderstood world where everyone comes to be entertained. But the real entertainment is watching people in the audience try to eat a purple Snack bar quietly during a dream sequence.

Take a scenic walk along the Hook Head peninsula to watch the sunset upon the shore. It's rumoured that if you stay here for too long a man who looks like a timeless old tree in a Wexford jersey will appear from beneath the rocks and make you share his bag of chips with him, claiming he won them in a battle at Vinegar Hill and won't eat them all himself.

### NIGHTLIFE

JD Norths is one of the favourite boozers of the natives. Purely because it sounds like the name of a shop that sells sports gear. Spider O'Brien's is another beloved local temple the locals find themselves piling into on a Sunday evening. Spider's got its name for their effort to improve the psychological wellbeing of the locals through radical exposure therapy. This pub serves great pints while making you face your fears. Once last orders have been called the owner presses a button under the bar that releases eight thousand tiny spiders across the establishment. The majority of the locals run out of the pub screaming, although it can be found that a few loyal patrons stay inside with spiders all over their face. It appears the cobwebs have them glued to their seats and they won't be getting up any time soon.

Namaste.

# COUNTY WICKLOW

Wicklow is a paradise for people who love hiking and pretending to be from Dublin just because they have internet connection. Wicklow used to be known as the Garden of Ireland, but ever since the council decided to cut all the trees down, the more fitting name for Wicklow would be the patio of Portobello.

# Top five things you don't want to miss:

### 1. The north Wicklow–D4 paradox

Everyone from Blessington wants to be from Donnybrook, while everyone from Bray wants to be from Cabra. Apparently when you put Greystones into Google Maps it says *Did you mean south Dublin?*

### 2. Visiting Simon Harris

Even though he used to be the minister for health, his office is still above a Chinese takeaway in Wicklow town. Which is totally ironic. No one from Wicklow town is healthy.

### 3. Picking mushrooms in the Wicklow mountains

You'll come across interesting characters on the mountains during mushroom season. Usually lads from Sligo who get all of their information about the world from a podcast.

### 4. Observing the walker-swimmer-surfer dichotomy

In Wicklow, you're only allowed be three things. A walker, a swimmer or a surfer. You can be each of these things at different stages in your life, but you're not allowed be more than one at a time.

### 5. Waiting for the bus in west Wicklow

Just make sure you have a long movie downloaded onto your phone and carry a bottle of water with you in case you die of dehydration while waiting for your bus-shaped beacon of hope out of this godforsaken place, which most likely, will never arrive.

# Redcross

Redcross is a small village situated in the low, slowly rolling hills of Wicklow. Despite its name, Redcross is not the arbiter of safe conduct. It's the exact opposite of a hospital. If you were to fall and break your leg on one of these country roads, so few people live here that by the time someone found you, you'd be two birthdays older and incredibly accustomed to lying on the ground, wriggling and writhing in pain.

## Urban myths and legends

Like many other random villages in Ireland, there was a movie shot here for some weird reason. It was a film by J.B. Keane called *Durango*. I refuse to believe it's real. Durango sounds like the name of a knock-off designer perfume that got smuggled into the country and sold in one of the market stalls in town. Due to this film being shot here, the local Redcrossians act as if their lives are being recorded. They don't think they are, but they believe it's best to act that way, just in case. That's why there are only two shops and one pub in Redcross. Less choice, less chances to ruin everything. Plus, nobody ever complained about a lack of consumer choices on a film set. So the locals are just going with the flow, afraid to speak out.

The main source of tourism holding up the economy of Redcross is the River Valley Holiday Park. This is a scenic camping area in the hills that sees swarms of families come to force their children to enjoy nature. The tourists usually come from places in south Dublin, places where camping is but a distant, alien concept. To cater to their demographic, the River Valley Park socially constructs nature to make it palatable to people who are used to living in first-class comfort. Right beside the tents you'll find state of the art showers along with the best (and only) BBQ food in all of Redcross. There's even a magician there to entertain your kids so you don't have to. This was another experience the River Valley Park socially designed. Because if you found a magician in the wilderness who tried to entertain your children, it would be absolutely terrifying. It's believed if you stay up in the River Valley Park past the curfew Bigfoot will appear and when he takes off his Bigfoot mask it's actually Eamon Dunphy on stilts. He will never tell you what he's doing in the bigfoot suit, never mind explain why he's in Redcross in the middle of the night.

## NIGHTLIFE

Sometimes parents will accidentally wander out of the River Valley Park and stumble into Mickey Finn's; one of the only pubs in Redcross. The Southsiders who wander into this fine establishment see themselves as sociologists conducting ethnographical research, capturing the lives of the country people, while they watch on from a distance without talking to them. Allegedly there's a giant red button under the bar in this pub that shoots tourists back into the camping park; the button is only used for non-locals. The technology is pretty simple, all they have to do is ask for a cocktail. The nightlife here consists of locals drinking in this pub until Mickey decides to shut down the bar. It's at this point Mickey Finn's becomes Mickey Finished. The remainder of the night in Redcross is usually spent walking home in the dark.

Namaste.

# Bray

Bray is a seaside town that likes to socially distance itself from the rest of Wicklow, while remaining on the outside looking into the promised land of South County Dublin. So, for now, Bray will have to remain in Bray. Statistics show that Bray is what you get if you bought Greystones on Wish.com. The God of Bray, Hozier, invented a mountain and named it Bray Head, because he recognised that everyone in Bray has a massive head. It was then that the people of Bray began calling themselves Bray heads.

## Urban myths and legends

Inside Bray is Little Bray, which is the part of Bray that borders south Dublin but secretly wishes it was from the northside. Contrary to popular belief, eighteen million people live in Little Bray but you can't see most of them because they're so small that they're invisible to the naked eye. Little Bray is just Bray with a Napoleon complex. Just outside Little Bray is Big Tesco, which kind of sounds like the name of a rapper. Big Tesco is the ancient protector of Bray and is often where Bray heads will congregate for safety purposes.

Bray is home to the Bray Wanderers, the football club famous for being one of the lowest-ranked teams on FIFA. FIFA have been conspiring against Bray Wanderers for years by giving them harsh ratings because they know if Bray Wanderers had self-confidence, they would stop wandering around Bray and would actually start playing football.

The males of Bray only have two possible names, Larry or Chap, there are no other names in Bray. If you walk onto the seafront and shout either of these names every man on the seafront will turn around. There was one guy there a while ago called Bernard but he got suffocated.

The McDonald's in Bray is a multi-purpose unit. It also doubles as a town hall. Using touch screens to order your Eurosaver meal in this ancient castle means this is the only McDonald's in the world you can be in both the future and the past at the same time.

Bray is home to some of the best fighters in the world. Actually no, Katie Taylor is the only fighter in the world who's from Bray. Now everyone else here thinks they can fight just because they know her. It's believed that if you walk along the seafront at 3.45 a.m. and stand two metres away from the kiosk and say Katie Taylor's name three times and then spin around, Katie Taylor will appear behind the counter and hand you a Nutella crêpe.

Over the last few years Bray has undergone a drastic cultural shift, and the catalyst for this change was the Catalyst coffee. Before this gourmet café, Bray was trapped in a perpetual state of 2006, powered by DJ Cammy illegal raves, and full of Fred Perry-wearing teenagers with earrings from Topman, drinking Druids and fighting each other on back beach. Once Catalyst appeared on the seafront, these very same people started drinking kombucha and posting pictures of their salads on Insta with #blessed, which is absolutely terrifying.

People in Bray are very sensitive about their takeaways. If you don't profess your love for the food in Capri's or you so much as hint that Teddy's ice cream would melt if it were left out in the sun for too long, the Bray heads will actually kill you.

The economy of Bray is propelled by the power of Peter's Pizza. Peter is the spiritual leader of Bray, renowned for his courageous activities during Storm Ophelia when the country was on red alert and he filmed himself throwing pizza boxes into the blistering wind and offered a two-for-one Storm Ophelia special.

## NIGHTLIFE

The social fabric that has glued the people of Bray together is Koo. This is the only nightclub in Bray and is a multicultural universe in itself. The term 'Koo' is short for 'kangaroo' because this club is the only place in Bray that you'll find people who come home after not being able to hack Australia, bouncing up and down like a marsupial while talking at you about Sydney after a few pints. Like somehow wearing a fake shark tooth necklace and a few too many open buttons on your sweat-patched dress shirt makes you think you're better than everyone else just because you spent a few months as a plumber in a different hemisphere.

Namaste.

# Enniskerry

Enniskerry is a small village in Wicklow. The ancient paradox of this cosy enclave is that although no one has ever been to Enniskerry, everyone assumes that there are three or four Enniskerries in Ireland. Each one less interesting than the next. Stuffed at the foothills of the Wicklow Mountains, the magnificent wonder of nature is lost on them. No one in Enniskerry has ever climbed a hill. They all agree that it's far too dangerous. It would shake their strongly held belief that the world is flat.

## Urban myths and legends

It's well documented that Enniskerry is, randomly, a village where movies are made. Some scenes from *P.S. I Love You* were shot here back in 2007, along with the less famous movie entitled *Piss, I Love You,* shot using one camera live from the mouth of a famous politician that we can't mention because we don't want him to get the recognition he deserves for his sterling performance. In more recent years, Disney decided no one really lives in Enniskerry and decided to turn it into a Hollywood movie set for a children's movie called *Disenchanted,* much to the disenchantment of the locals who had very little say in the matter.

While Enniskerry made the transition from being a village nobody ever heard of to becoming a hotbed of aging millennials desperately trying to recapture their unhappy childhood under the guise of a Mickey Mouse hat and a failure to become an adult, Enniskerrians were gaslighted into believing that their beloved village was always sponsored by Disney. The Enniskerrians were taught that they lacked the inherent free will necessary to break free from the iron grip of Mickey Mouse. Slaves to the relentless rhythm of the *Frozen* soundtrack. This conspiracy was allegedly backed up by RTÉ, who have reportedly been in cahoots with Disney for millennia. RTÉ created a piece on the 6 o'clock news showing supposedly happy Enniskerry locals in vehement support of Disney turning their village into a movie set. Many are unaware that the editors of RTÉ are so skilled at what they do that they can chop and change a camera reel to artificially manufacture genuine happiness.

All in all, there's not much else to say about Enniskerry. There's a roundabout here and the legend goes that if you rip enough wheelies on a bike while wearing bootcut jeans, you'll get so dizzy that you'll transport yourself into Spar, which is the only other place in Enniskerry you'll find actual signs of human life.

## NIGHTLIFE

No.
   Namaste.

## Greystones

Greystones is an upper-class coastal town in County Wicklow. Greystones is divided into two categories, people who pretend to be from Bray to sound less posh and people who think Greystones is an honourary member of the region of Dublin 4.

### Urban myths and legends

Greystones used to be a barren wasteland but now it's a barren wasteland that has become overgrown with trendy cafes, specialist food stores and three ice-cream shops on the main street. Greystones is a harbinger of the post-industrial apocalypse. A safe haven for chain stores and franchises that blunt the character of the area, eventually turning it into a gigantic Starbucks.

Aunty Nellie's sweet shop is one of the most iconic spots in Greystones. No one has ever seen Aunty Nellie in the flesh. It's rumoured that the shop is secretly run by the lads who own the Happy Pear. At this point, the allegations can not be confirmed or denied.

Meridian Point shopping centre was unveiled to the Greystonians in 2004. A meridian point is a point on the compass. In this case, it points towards Donnybrook. There used to be a Carphone Warehouse shop here and a homeware store, so people would only ever come here if they smashed their smartphone or broke a chair. Now it's basically just a hairdressers. No one ever goes there because people from Greystones all have bowl cuts that don't grow. There's a nice Indian restaurant that overlooks the shopping centre. Giving the Greystonians a dinner and a view. They usually say something like 'They should really replace that shopping centre with a Croke Park-sized Fallon & Byrne's'. Although they'd probably say Lansdowne Road, because Croke Park is on the Northside.

There are more coffee shops in Greystones than there are women out walking their white fluffy dogs on the local beach every morning. Thousands. They say if flat whites were abolished tomorrow morning, everyone in Greystones would fall asleep and never wake up. Their levels of privilege are so exhausting that they wouldn't be able to support the weight of their wallets and would keel over on the cobblestones.

Greystones is ruled by the Happy Pear. The twins set up shop in the town thousands of years ago, handing out kale smoothies and superiority complexes. The Happy Pear used to be called The Sad Bananas but changed their name because it made everyone think they were rotten.

Greystones beach is a sociological study that has been puzzling astrologists for centuries. But that's only because astrologists don't know anything about sociology. On a sunny day at the beach, you'll find a wide range of human beings. You'll find the Greystones natives, easy to spot because they're the ones sea-swimming and taking pictures of it. Then you'll find the lads from Bray. You'll know who they are because they'll be the ones drinking cans while staring out at the sea and starting on each other. They never take their clothes off to go for a swim because they're ashamed of their lack of tattoos. The ancient rule states one can not look into the eyes of a Bray head for more than 2.3 seconds without them asking 'What the fuck you lookin at Larry?'.

# NIGHTLIFE

Mrs Robinson's is the pub where successful people over thirty go to network with each other and pretend to get drunk. If you come in here under the age of twenty-six and don't know anything about cryptocurrency they will send you off in a cab. The Burnaby Pub is home to all the older Greystones residents. The farmers who lived here before Greystones gentrification all drink here. The only place for the younger Greystonians to drink and socialise with each other is in Bray. No one ever ends up there due to their fear of public transport. And Bray.

Namaste.